"*He Knows Your Name* is a must-read for women and men alike. I've known Paige Allen for many years, and she articulates straight from God's Word those sentiments that we all sense arising in our hearts: *Does He see me? Does He know me? Will He be there in my need?* This book hits the mark and addresses these questions of the heart by exploring some of the more obscure women who encountered God in the pages of Scripture. Paige Allen is a rising voice in our nation today!"

Randy Boyd, executive director, Prepare International

"Get the tissues ready. Paige Allen brilliantly takes nameless woman in the Bible and somehow allows us to see ourselves identifying with their struggles and pain. Using her own vulnerability and transparency she brings us besides still waters and assures us that He knows our name."

Maria Durso, pastor and author, Saints Church

"You are blessed to have this book in your hand. All of us feel unseen at times, and this book does a great job of unwrapping those moments, encouraging us, and filling us with glimpses of God's love. Paige so clearly and beautifully portrays Jesus's heart through the pages of *He Knows Your Name*. We've known Paige for nearly twenty years and have seen her minister to different groups of people worldwide, and her voice has consistently spoken God's love and presence to a variety of listeners. Paige has a credible voice that should be heard. We highly encourage all to read this book."

Dwayne and Leslie Weehunt, cofounders,
SOS International Ministries

"As a businesswoman, TEDx speaker, pastor's wife, and mom, I've come across women from every sector of society and know at our core we are all asking similar questions about the value we bring to this world. In *He Knows Your Name*, Paige Allen speaks to these questions and brings actual hope! Women will walk away from this book with a new confidence that they matter because Jesus not only sees them but knows them too!"

Lynette Lewis, TEDx speaker, business consultant, author

"I can't wait for you to read this book! Paige gives all of us permission to identify the ways we feel nameless and yet are seen and known. Relevant and widely applicable, this book will have you reflecting on Jesus and the very intimate encounters He longs to have with you."

Laura Brandenburg, author of *Not Forgotten: Unraveling Questions of Faith and Infertility*

"Paige masterfully reminds us that the birthright of everyone in Christ is this: knowing we are His and He is ours—no matter how the world defines us. As you read, you'll laugh, you'll cry, and I bet you'll know and love Jesus even more than when you started."

Sara Lubbers, author of *Always Love* and *Our God Wins*

"If you've ever asked yourself the question *Where do I belong?*, especially as a woman in the kingdom, this book is a safe haven filled with women who have asked that same question. You will be equipped, challenged, encouraged, and inspired to surrender to Jesus all over again."

Zahriya Zachary, Bethel Music

"Paige Allen offers a fresh perspective by weaving together biblical and personal stories. You feel like she is talking directly to you! Deep spiritual truths are shared in easy-to-understand ways that leave you encouraged and challenged. Almost like being wrapped in a warm, comfy blanket. It is hard to put the book down!"

Dr. Kathy Crockett, Kathy Crockett + Co

HE
KNOWS
YOUR
NAME

HE KNOWS YOUR NAME

HOW 7 NAMELESS WOMEN OF THE BIBLE REVEAL CHRIST'S LOVE FOR YOU

PAIGE ALLEN

BETHANYHOUSE
a division of Baker Publishing Group
Minneapolis, Minnesota

Published by Bethany House Publishers
Minneapolis, Minnesota
www.bethanyhouse.com

Bethany House Publishers is a division of
Baker Publishing Group, Grand Rapids, Michigan

Printed in the United States of America

Library of Congress Cataloging-in-Publication Data
Names: Allen, Paige, author.
Title: He knows your name : how 7 nameless women of the Bible reveal Christ's love for you / Paige Allen.
Description: Minneapolis : Bethany House Publishers, a division of Baker Publishing Group, 2023. | Includes bibliographical references.
Identifiers: LCCN 2023018331 | ISBN 9780764241758 (paperback) | ISBN 9780764242311 (casebound) | ISBN 9781493443840 (ebook)
Subjects: LCSH: Women in the Bible. | God (Christianity)—Love.
Classification: LCC BS575 .A447 2023 | DDC 226/.0922—dc23/eng/20230616
LC record available at https://lccn.loc.gov/2023018331

The author is represented by the literary agency of Punchline Agency, LLC.

Baker Publishing Group publications use paper produced from sustainable forestry practices and post-consumer waste whenever possible.

23 24 25 26 27 28 29   7 6 5 4 3 2 1

For my mom,
who showed me it's okay to wrestle with belonging
because on the other side is the knowing—
He sees us and that is always enough.

CONTENTS

INTRODUCTION

What's in a Name?

I'm a pastor's kid who grew up in the late '80s and early '90s. During Halloween, many evangelical churches instead hosted Harvest Festivals, Trunk or Treats, or, in our church's case, an annual Hallelujah Night! There were games, candy, a chili cook-off, and awards handed out for the best Bible character costume. A couple of years into trying to compete for this coveted award, I realized my options were fairly limited as a girl trying to dress as a Bible character. In a sea of Marys and Queen Esthers, there was usually someone who stood out because they did something extra creative, like the one girl who dressed up as Jezebel (spicy), or the large homeschool family dressed as the Fruit of the Spirit, which felt unfair since they had nine children (wowzers) and I only have two sisters (what were our options—Father, Son, and Holy Ghost?).

Boys on the other hand, in my opinion, had so many more options. They could come as David with an awesome slingshot, Noah with a basketful of stuffed animals, or even Jesus! And let's be honest, it almost feels wrong to beat someone who dresses up as Jesus.

One year, at the ripe age of ten, I was determined to win. I tried to think big and break the mold because I had my heart set on walking away with that year's prize: a twenty-dollar gift card to Toys "R" Us, which would go toward my dream purchase of a Nintendo Game Boy and my desire to dominate at Tetris. So, I pitched idea after idea to my parents with little avail. They vetoed my idea of going as Eve with some well-placed leaves, and they could not figure out how to construct a Tower of Babel, even though I had architecture plans ready to go. After returning to the drawing board, I decided that if I could not beat the boys, then I would join them. I would dress up as John the Baptist.

Let me tell you, I went all out that year. I found some strange matted fur in my grandmother's closet that we molded into clothing. I ratted my hair, drew on a beard, found a jar of honey and a giant walking stick, and perfected my best imitation of a manly stride. When I walked into the Hallelujah Night, I noticed the stares. I'm not sure if people were amazed or horrified at how well I'd transformed into the wild man from the wilderness. I'm proud to say that I won the costume contest with honey in hand, ignoring the snickers from jealous boys and beating out a fierce Samson and someone covered in plastic frogs, attempting to be a plague.

But I didn't walk away that night with only a Toys "R" Us gift card. I also walked away from that experience with a gnawing in my gut that there had to be more stories about brave and courageous women in the Bible. Although I couldn't fully articulate it at the age of ten, I felt sad that there weren't more dress-up options for me as a girl. I loved Ruth, Deborah, Mary, and Esther, but these women seemed tame and were so few in comparison to David, Noah, Joshua, Moses, Peter, Paul, Gideon, Samson, Jacob, Abraham, Jonah, and John (care for me to go on?). Where were the women? Were they all busy inside tents with food and babies? Were there any women present during Jesus's ministry that I didn't know about? Were there any "wild" women who were bold and brave, maybe not as crazy as wilderness-wandering-and-locust-eating John the Baptist, but women who were desperate for an encounter with the man from Nazareth? Women a little like me?

This preacher's kid grew up, went to college and seminary, got married, read through the Gospels a few times, and wound up working in her dad's church (even judging the chili cook-off at our Hallelujah Night, which was renamed Family Fall Fest to stay relevant). I remained on the lookout as I opened my Bible for brave women to learn from, and although I've been captivated by the stories of Mary, Martha, Jael, and Anna the prophetess, more often than not, I kept circling back to the stories of women who didn't appear to get a lot of airtime but who obviously had significant and even life-altering encounters with the Savior.

Years ago, I wrote a Bible study and included a lesson from the life of the woman with the issue of blood. After that teaching session, a lady named Michelle mentioned to me that she was captivated by women like the one I'd just taught on—women who were without a name, nameless women, in Scripture. She was currently diving deep into 2 Kings 4 and the miraculous story of Elisha when he encountered a poor widow on the brink of losing her sons to creditors. As Michelle shared her excitement, I couldn't shake the phrase *nameless women*, and I realized that I too was drawn to their stories! These brave women littered my sermons and made me pause as I read the Bible because their faith and willingness to be a little "wild" was flat-out inspiring. Stories like that of the woman with the issue of blood caused me to think about determined faith, and the story of the Syrophoenician woman, who broke numerous cultural boundaries as she begged at the table of Jesus, gripped me and caused me to take inventory of my own life. Had I ever been as desperate as these nameless women for a touch from Jesus?

As I pondered that conversation with Michelle, I decided to revisit these stories, especially the ones found in Matthew, Mark, Luke, and John—the stories of nameless women who met Jesus face-to-face. As I studied, I wrestled with the simple fact that these women were somewhat anonymous. Their identity was hidden, their background left to our imagination, and their future a mystery. In some ways, this frustrated me. Their anonymity highlights the marginalization of women during Bible times, and in all honesty, my research of these women began with plenty of arguments with God, asking Him, *Why don't they even get a name in here?!*

But as I continued to dive into these stories and preach about them in various situations, I found my indignation lessening and hope rising as I saw over and over how their namelessness didn't define them: Jesus didn't see these women as a quota or photo op but rather drew near to them with love and freedom. These stories are in the Bible for a reason. They aren't throwaway moments, even if the women remain unnamed to this day. If anything, I find these women are reflections of the anonymous and sometimes hidden lives many women lead today.

We've all been there, whether standing in a crowd of people or alone in our homes, wondering if what we do matters. We feel nameless—overwhelmed and overlooked. We stand in the shadow of our Mount Everest laundry piles or look at the paper that litters our desks, wondering if anyone actually knows or cares about our day, our life. We open Instagram in hopes of validation or at least distraction but wind up in despair as the merry-go-round of pretty faces and perfect homes leaves us feeling small and unimportant. We find ourselves teetering on a balance beam of wanting to scream out something profound yet questioning the significance of our voice. We look around our hurting world, hoping our little light is making a difference yet feeling that light flicker more than shine.

We want to be known.

We want to make Him known.

But we question. We question our significance and overanalyze how to live in a way that is both authentic and impactful. We spend time rehashing old rejections, remembering when we stood before the in-crowd receiving cold shoulders instead of open arms. Or we opt for numbness, choosing to binge a new show or navigate our days on autopilot, because let's be honest, it's easier to fake a smile than to feel the grief attached to dead dreams and unmet expectations. We also listen to the lies of the enemy that say we have little to offer beyond making sandwiches and carpooling kids, assisting others and working behind the scenes, whispers that point out our flaws and failures while highlighting the accolades of others.

And yet, even with this list of sad stories and what-if scenarios that takes up space in our brains, *we still hope*. You've picked up this book because even in the questions, I know there is a flicker of hope deep within you that your life matters and is seen by a good God. Like me, you are tired of living on a seesaw of emotions, unsure of what you'll feel next. You are ready for security and truth and clarity on who you are.

As I talk to women at my church and around the country, I'm finding many who are desperate to connect with the Lord in a fresh and personal way. Women want to learn to hear the voice of Jesus, to experience His presence, and to know Him in a tangible, settled way that reminds us that though the earth may quake, there is One who is constant—and He knows us by name.

Isaiah 43:1–3 (emphasis added) is a beautiful promise directed to the nation of Israel, and I believe it is a reflection of God's heart toward us today:

"Do not be afraid, for I have ransomed you.
I have called you by name; you are mine.
When you go through deep waters,
I will be with you.
When you go through rivers of difficulty,
you will not drown.
When you walk through the fire of oppression,
you will not be burned up;
the flames will not consume you.
For I am the LORD, your God,
the Holy One of Israel, your Savior."

On the days we feel disoriented, forgotten, or face-to-face with a raging fire, we can open the pages of Scripture and find that these promises are not words flung randomly in the wind, but they literally embody the person of Jesus. Jesus went out of His way to pause, to listen to, and to redeem marginalized women. They were nameless women, walking through deep waters of difficulty and fires of oppression, and He was there. He knew them and called them His own.

If Jesus went out of His way to listen to nameless women in the Gospels, then He is listening to us today.

He is listening to you.

This book is an exploration of what it means to be seen, heard, and known by Jesus. We will look at seven different encounters in the Gospels where Jesus connects with nameless women, deeply examining the stories that changed their lives. I weave my own personal stories throughout these gospel narratives because I believe Jesus not only spoke to these women, but He is moving and speaking to women today. As you read about His interactions with me, my friends, and women like the widow with two mites, I believe you will get a truer glimpse of how good and loving our God is. These unknown women encountered Jesus in such a beautiful and personal way that they each moved from a posture of dejection and desperation to one of faith and confidence. When these women encountered Jesus, they encountered hope.

Hope is waiting for you too.

A.W. Tozer said, "We can never know who or what we are till we know at least something of what God is."[1]

The truth is that we are known only as we know Him.

This truth became real to me in the spring of 2000. I was engaged and planning my upcoming wedding. When I took a break from choosing cakes and bridesmaid dresses, I found myself melting down with a wise friend over the issue that my name would soon change. Something about that reality not only unsettled me but made me question my identity, purpose, and future. For all my life, I had been Paige White. This name connected me to my parents, my heritage, and I had made Paige White look pretty good! People liked Paige White. *I* liked Paige White. But who would Paige Allen be? This new last name was foreign on my tongue. It felt forced, and although I was ecstatic to marry this man, I just wasn't so sure about taking his name. This name change represented an unknown future, and at my core I felt like I was being invited to change something essential about myself, but I wasn't sure if I wanted to accept the invitation. Fears that I'd long covered up surfaced with a vengeance. I started to question my value, my purpose, my friendships, and if I might be making a huge mistake marrying this man who was my exact opposite in

1. A.W. Tozer, *The Knowledge of the Holy: The Attributes of God: Their Meaning in the Christian Life* (San Francisco: HarperOne, 2009), 28.

personality. It was just a name change, and yet it seemed to unlock a door to questions I needed to face.

My wise friend said I had to get a sense of peace about this change and encouraged me to stop the mind games and try to ask God what was going on at a deeper level. I left her office and found myself in a rose garden, sitting on a section of steps surrounded by hundreds of thorny stems that had yet to bloom. Determined not to leave that garden until I had some sort of answer, I paced, journaled, cried, and found myself asking the Lord about more than a name change—I was actually asking Him about *my* identity. When the questions dried up and I sat with an open heart and unclenched fists, the Holy Spirit gently spoke to my heart. His words were simple. "Paige, you are my child."

These five words were plain yet revelatory because they were spoken directly to my heart. With the name *child*, I felt as if God was imparting security and a sense of belonging that transcended any name change I might face. I was waking up to an uncomplicated identity that carried weight because it was attached to a good God who had things under control. More than Paige White versus Paige Allen, I was His child. He knew my name. That reality carried substance, purpose, and an authority I knew He was inviting me to discover.

Although a name change still sounded strange to my ear, I left the garden that day with an expectation that something really good was around the corner. I was excited to get to know Paige Allen, and I had an awareness that in order to settle into my identity as God's child, I needed to discover Him as my Father. It was as if I had a promise that if I'd continue to lean into His voice, scour His Word, and get to know Him, my identity would only grow.

That year of engagement became one of encountering the Lord as my Father and seeing this promise of a secured identity bloom in my life. I read the Bible with new eyes, and as I read verses like Romans 8:15, "Instead, you received God's Spirit when he adopted you as his own children. Now we call him, 'Abba, Father,'" I had aha moments when I not only gained greater knowledge of who God is as My Father but also became more confident in who I was as His child. It was connected! Discovering the name of God as Father allowed me to move into a new season with joy and freedom as His child.

We become known as we get to know Him.

Now, as a culture, we love to focus on ourselves, and most people are on a quest to gain greater clarity on their identity. We want to feel known, and many of us want to *be* known. It's a different story, but even my eleven-year-old asked for her own YouTube channel for Christmas. We resist the concept of a nameless existence, which is why the self-help industry brings in over eleven billion dollars each year. I love a good self-help book, but I've also experienced the reality that running after mantras or new habits often leaves me wanting, and there is nothing that solidifies a sense of being known quite like discovering in greater detail the One who created me.

Each of the nameless gospel women that we explore in this book has her own movement moment where she transitions from an unsure, hidden woman in the background of the story into a woman who is seen, valued, and in many instances sent out to transform her world. The pivotal point within each narrative is the life-giving encounter she has with Jesus. As I began to study these stories, it was as if I began to see within each one a new aspect of Jesus, an attribute or "name," if you will, that was on full display in the interactions He had with each anonymous woman. And as I watched these nameless women transform within a span of a few verses, it got me to thinking: What would happen if we, if you, took the time to discover who God really is? Could transformation in our lives (like that of the nameless women) be as simple as seeing and encountering Jesus in a new light? What would life look like if we actually believed that He is the God who sees us? How would we parent or treat our friends if we had a radical revelation that He is our shepherd and advocate? Might our worries and fears be lessened with the soul-deep belief that He alone is our peace and protector? Would we no longer feel nameless? Would we stop caring so much about being known? Would we begin to use our voices? Could we, like the woman at the well, wind up transforming a community?

This book is broken into seven sections that take a closer look at seven brave but anonymous women who encountered Jesus in the Gospels. Each section has two chapters: one that shines a light on the narrative of the nameless woman and one that looks at a name or characteristic of God that Jesus exemplifies in the same story.

We will first look at the story from her perspective. This includes trying to understand what was happening culturally and relating her obstacles or lessons to the modern-day issues we face. Then in the second chapter of each section we will get to know Jesus as shepherd, advocate, living water, Father, and more!

Whether you are surrounded by the masses (maybe you are a famous YouTuber whom my child adores) or reading in your home while little ones tug for your attention, it is my prayer that these words remind you that you are not alone. There have been women who have gone before us who faced disease, poverty, injustice, and shame, and because of *one man* who walked into their world, they were reminded that there is always hope. They were seen by Him. They were set free by Him. They were released into purpose by Him. Some were corrected by Him. All were loved by Him. We don't know their names, but their stories live on, and in His presence they became women whom the whole world would know.

It is also my prayer that you walk away from this book knowing that the Jesus who went out of His way to connect with, heal, and fight for nameless women in the Gospels is the same Jesus who listens and speaks to you today. May the chaos or hiddenness of your current season and the questions of your heart melt away as you meet Jesus in a new way and are awakened to the truth that He knows your name. Because when you are known, it changes everything!

STOP
IN THE
NAME
OF LOVE

The Woman
with the Issue of Blood

Luke 8:40–56

1

A Woman Reaches

I was pitching this book to potential publishers when I received a concerning call from my dear college friend Angel. Through tears, she told me her marriage was over, she was a horrible mother, and she was questioning the value she brought to her family and any area of life, for that matter. She had battled postpartum depression for a few years now, but her words hit my ears like alarms. They sounded so far from the Angel I knew.

I met Angel my very first day at college. My parents had just said their good-byes, and I found myself in a new city, weeping alone in my new dorm room. I cried for a solid hour before I realized I didn't want to be the sad girl who cries alone in her dorm room. So I wiped my eyes, blew my nose, did a once-over in the mirror, and put on my bravest smile. I stepped into the long hallway and knocked on the door directly across from my room. Imagine my surprise when that door opened up to another girl wiping away her tears and looking at me with a puzzled expression on her face. Her name was Wendy, and we decided to knock on every door down that long hallway, inviting everyone to go get ice cream.

Angel was only two doors down from my room, and instead of greeting us with tears, we were greeted with blaring '80s music and a smile that lit up the campus. Angel was definitely on board to go get ice cream, and from that day forward, the three of us—Paige, Wendy, and Angel—became a tight-knit crew. All of my best college memories include Wendy and Angel. They helped set me up with my husband, Josh, and we were bridesmaids in one another's weddings. We had more honest conversations over ice cream than I can count, we've gotten into trouble a time or two, and these two are the friends who leave me doubled over in laughter with a side-eye and smirk.

Angel is one of my people. She is my fun friend. She is my brave friend. She is the friend with an inappropriate question ready to go at any minute, and gosh I love it when she asks that question because I'm dying to know the answer too, even if I'm too shy to ask.

So this phone call I received made me sit up, immediately call Wendy, and make plans with her to travel to Tulsa within weeks to go check on our friend. The weekend we arrived was different from other girls' weekends we'd had in the past. This was not a time to sight-see and try new foods—from the moment we got in Angel's car at the airport, we were accosted with tears and rants and the heartache of a friend who felt lost and alone even though she was surrounded by so many who loved her. I was nervous and wasn't sure if I had the answers she sought. We talked and we cried and we talked some more. Angel's words seemed to go in a circle, and I was left frustrated by the way she was thinking. She slept a lot too. She chose to stay in the hotel to nap while Wendy and I got pedicures. She asked if we could go home early after dinner so she could go to bed, even though we *always* stayed up late when we were together. It was odd. It wasn't the Angel we knew. Something just seemed off. This didn't seem like only marriage troubles or even postpartum depression.

One afternoon as Angel drove down the winding street of Lewis Avenue, she began talking in a shame spiral. She recounted to us the many ways she was failing her family and how she believed she wasn't cutting it in most areas of life. She pulled me into the conversation, comparing her life to my own, wishing that she was the one in ministry and writing books, wondering how her life had gotten so off track from the plans in her mind. I sat next to her in the passenger's seat and turned to face her.

I've been guilty of talking badly about myself, but Angel spoke with venom in her voice, berating every area of her life, and I knew in my spirit it needed to stop. So as she continued to drive with her face pointed forward, I began to recount the Angel I knew. "Angel, I know this is a hard season, but you've got to remember who you are! Let me tell you about who I see when I see you." And I went for it. I reminded her of her infectious laughter and her ability to make everyone feel like they are her best friend. I reminded her of stories of her bravery and how she loves her boys fiercely. I went on and on and on, and as I did, tears silently ran down her face.

She smiled and wiped her tears, thanking me for my kind words, but it was as if she also brushed my words off like crumbs that had landed in her lap. She couldn't take the honest praise in, so the words slid to the floor rather than taking up residence in her heart.

The next day, she dropped Wendy and me off at the airport, and we stood together under the Tulsa sky, scratching our heads and literally saying to one another, "What's really going on? What are we missing?"

Wendy and I decided to send daily text messages to Angel, reminding her of who she is and of God's goodness toward her. And we received nice replies back for a couple of months, but then she went silent.

Isn't silence the worst?

When you are hoping for an answer, silence is deafening and often infuriating. It speaks its own kind of language, and when we listen in, we can hear the voices of our past pointing out some of our greatest fears. That small voice that taps into the old wounds, telling you that you will always be chosen last or that your presence is only needed so long as it is "useful." Silence whispers you're unworthy of that person's time or love, and if we are not careful, we create entire scenarios in our imagination where we stand before the crowds we most want to join and hear the verdict that our presence is unimportant or a nuisance.

Although Angel wasn't trying to send those messages, I received them all the same, and I've realized over the years that anytime I don't receive the feedback I crave, from work or my husband or even my children, I begin to question my value and whether or not anyone sees me for who I really am. I can begin to believe that I'm nothing more than the food I make, the rides I give to children bickering in the backseat, and the events I organize at work. And it doesn't matter if God is sitting next to me in the car, reminding me through His Word that I am beloved, because in order to be known and seen, I must be willing to listen and believe.

Silence wields power not only when it's directed our way but especially when it is forced upon our voice or presence. I'll never forget watching the Oprah interview with Prince Harry and Meghan Markle a few years ago. They were sitting underneath a canopy of flowers, sharing about their time in the royal circles, when Oprah asked Meghan this question:

"Were you silent, or were you silenced?"[1] I made a small gasp because the question hit so close to my heart. There have been times when I felt silenced—asked to step aside or hold my opinion—but there have also been occasions, more than I'd like to admit, when I chose to be silent, to hold back my voice, because I was unsure of how it would be received.

I'm not sure if receiving silence or being silenced causes me more turmoil, but when any type of silence creeps in, I tend to look for an exit, or just some way to fill the gap. In Angel's life, I would later discover that the silence was a result of a hidden battle with demons I cannot fathom. So the silence was not a message for me so much as a consequence of her pain and shame. I saw her actions as her giving me the silent treatment, when in reality she was being silenced by an enemy I had yet to encounter.

I know that I'm not the only woman frustrated by silence. I've sat with young women from conservative denominations who have cried about the fact that they are unwelcome to use their voice when they have so much to offer. I have run alongside women who have secret desires to start a business or ministry but believe their husbands or extended families only see them as capable of spending money and cooking food. I have cuddled my own daughters as tears pooled in their eyes after hearing through the grapevine that they were excluded from an invitation, wondering what they were lacking in order to be invited into the cool crowd. What about you? What is harder—receiving silence or feeling that you need to be silent?

I often wonder how many unnamed women in Scripture felt enraged yet helpless at the reality that their existence was

1. "Prince Harry, Meghan reveal struggles behind royal rift in Oprah interview," YouTube video, 0:22, posted by CBS News: The National on March 7, 2021, https://www.youtube.com/watch?v=Wx4Vpm1KzSY.

often silenced. They had little to no voice in whom they would marry, or in any gifts and talents they held beyond their ability to birth and raise children. They had no voice when it came to financial decisions, and their very existence was considered expendable—especially when there was no male relative willing to advocate for them.

We see this issue play out so clearly in the story of the woman with the issue of blood, found in the gospels of Matthew, Mark, and Luke. This woman is alone, rejected, sidelined, and without any male relative to fight for her. She is also nameless. This woman most likely was handed down a looming sentence of isolation and embarrassment. According to Leviticus 15:25, she is deemed "unclean" for as long as she continues to bleed. She has racked up twelve years so far, and the Bible tells us that she's shelled out every penny to her name, desperate to find a cure. But even though she may be broke on this day that we meet her in Scripture, she is also determined to find a way to break free from this unending cycle of despair and pain.

The reality that the world has turned its back on her is specifically displayed in great detail in Luke's recounting of her story, found in Luke 8:40–56. Her story is sandwiched inside the story of another woman, a girl really, a girl the same age as the number of years this woman has bled, a twelve-year-old girl.

Side note—when you see similar parallels or details like this in the Bible, like this woman who has bled for twelve years and a little girl who is only twelve years old, *it's not a coincidence.* It's an invitation to stop and examine. Are there any other similarities between these two nameless women? What about any differences?

You know what stands out most to me as I compare these two women side by side? Although they share the same gender and the number twelve in their descriptions, I believe the truth is that these two women could not be more different.[2]

The little girl came from a wealthy and well-known family. In fact, we discover that her father was not nameless. He is known. He is Jairus. His was a name that people recognized and revered. He was a ruler of the synagogue, a righteous man. I wonder if he was one who helped hand down the sentence to the woman who bled, so that she must live her days away from those she loved.

I'm not sure if he was a kind and just ruler, but we do get a glimpse of the fact that he is a good father. His little girl is sick, and in a society when girls were sometimes discarded, he was willing to humble himself, literally falling to the ground in a manner that rulers would eschew, to fight for his daughter's life. He pleads with Jesus, acknowledging His authority in the midst of both fanfare and skepticism among his community, and asks for help. He's willing to fight and beg for his daughter. This little girl has a man in her corner. She has a dad who loves her.

In contrast, the woman who bleeds has no one. No one to fight, no one to beg, no man in sight. She is alone. It is silent. And so she musters up her own strength and pushes through that loud and restless crowd. I envision her giving herself the best Brené Brown pep talk about vulnerability and courage as she presses through the throngs of people. She has one small mission: to touch His clothing. Get in and get out. Hope for healing but stay under the radar.

And she does it! Scripture says that she touches the hem of Jesus's garment and is immediately healed. She feels the

2. I heard about this idea of comparing the woman with the issue of blood and Jairus's daughter from Dwayne Weehunt, founder of SOS International. He preached a life-changing message about these two women over a decade ago as I sat in a room filled with young women in the nation of India. I've studied and preached on this passage from this comparison and contrast angle on several occasions, but this transformative truth originated from him. Thank you, Dwayne.

bleeding stop. Can you imagine the relief and overwhelming joy that must have broken through the walls built up to protect her heart from another disappointment? She is healed! She can breathe. She can hope.

She begins to pull away, to try to blend back in with the crowd, when Jesus asks, "Who touched me?" And no one answers. Silence.

She shuts her mouth and looks around. Remember, she's not even supposed to be here. She has been labeled unclean, so anyone who touched her or came into her presence has been defiled. If it's discovered that she has broken out of her isolation, the ramifications no doubt would be devastating. And so she is silent. Eyes darting, heart pounding, mind racing, she is trying to sort out what is about to happen.

Jesus stops. He is not moving on. Peter tries to break the awkwardness like any good extrovert, reminding Jesus that a lot of people have touched Him. But Jesus is insistent. This touch was different.

Silence.

We aren't told how long the silence lasts, but in that silence, I believe something shifts.

The silences of God are always different from the silences of man. My friend Eric says, "God is always doing more than one thing at a time." God is unlimited by time and space, but more importantly, He sees beyond surface need to the deep places of our hearts. And when we are in the midst of pain or loss or even silence, He is at work.

I believe Jesus was at work that day, and although the woman had a simple agenda of getting physical healing from Him, He had an additional plan of bringing her healing at a soul level.

As this woman fights for herself, alone, desperate, and in the literal shadow of a good daddy fighting for his daughter, Jesus stops her because He has more.

When she realizes she can't stay hidden, she breaks the silence, and in complete vulnerability in front of a crowd of people, she tells Jesus her story. Her sickness, her rejection, and her determination to touch Him in order to be healed. I imagine her with tears running down her cheeks, rambling nervously as she told her story. I know I would.

And when all of her words are used up, Jesus responds. His words are simple, but look closely at how He begins: "Daughter." He calls her *daughter.*

And with one simple word, He trades her issue for identity. She is given a name. He fills the silence with comfort. She is *His daughter.* Like the sick little girl whose loving father still stands at Jesus's side, she too now has someone in her corner. His name is Jesus. He aligns Himself with her and calls her His own. And with this new name, Jesus brings another layer of healing to her soul.

He also makes a statement to her community. She is not to be rejected, and she is no longer alone. She has a man who will fight for her. A man who will stop crowds for her. A man who calls her daughter. A daughter has a place in a family, a seat at the table, and a connection with others that cannot be broken. She is no longer to be placed on the outskirts of her community. She belongs.

If you learn nothing else from the nameless women in the Gospels, let this truth sink down into the vulnerable places of your heart—Jesus sees you, is willing to stop the noise for you, and gives you the name your heart most needs to hear.

2

A Father Heals

I was tucking my then four-year-old daughter, Selah, into bed one night when she looked at me with her big blue eyes and proclaimed, "Mom, I really want to be a flower girl!" I began to ask her more about this request while simultaneously cataloging our friends and family to ascertain if there was any way she might get her wish. I could not think of a single person in our lives who was on the verge of marriage or even engagement and would have any reason to ask Selah, so I began my best to explain that although this was a wonderful dream, not everyone gets to be a flower girl.

She was up to the task of debate and explained her reasons why she needed to be a flower girl. First, this wasn't just wishful thinking but her *greatest dream ever*! And didn't her father and I say she could be anything she put her mind to? Uh . . . yes, we did. Second, all of her cousins had been flower girls, so surely she would be next. I was about to refute this claim when I again went down the list in my mind and realized she was correct. All of her cousins had carried petals down the aisle.

I took a deep breath and tried my best to explain that her cousins were in weddings of people they were really close to, like uncles and babysitters. I tried to soften the blow as I pushed back her hair and said, "Not all little girls get to be flower girls, but you would be an amazing one." I thought I was swaying her and watched as her nose scrunched up in thought, when out of her lips came this question: "What about you, Mom? Were you a flower girl?" Knife to my heart. Oh, how I wanted to stand in solidarity with her and my points of reason, but I had to confess, "Yes, I was a flower girl when I was five years old."

I was at a loss for what to say to this precocious girl, so I fell back on my pastor go-to and found myself saying, "Well, why don't you pray about it?" As soon as those words left my mouth, I desperately wanted to reel them back in for fear that her prayer wouldn't come true, but she took me up on it. Right there in that moment, she prayed with sincerity I've rarely heard. She closed her eyes, folded her hands, and began to pray, "Jesus, would you *please* make me a flower girl? I will do a good job throwing the petals, and it is what I want so, so much."

Her simple prayer brought tears to my eyes, but rather than lingering, I gave her a kiss, tucked her snugly in bed, and left her room to find my husband, Josh. He was watching television, and as I flopped down on the couch next to him, I sighed and said, "Well, I think I just set up our four-year-old for her first disappointment in God."

As I lay in bed that night, I couldn't shake the flower girl conversation. It wasn't so much the possibility of setting my child up for disappointment that was rolling through my mind, but rather her childlike ability to name so clearly and with such confidence what she wanted. She wanted to be a flower girl. Period. She didn't need to preface her request or give a disclaimer just in case rejection or embarrassment was on the other side. She was the epitome of vulnerability as she bared her deepest dream for me to hear. And when I suggested asking God about it, there was no hesitation, no calculating the probability of receiving her request, no self-protection or even assumption of disappointment.

She wanted and she asked and she believed.

I wondered, when was the last time that I lived with so much freedom and boldness? When was the last time I named (without disclaimer or preface) what I wanted? I too was once a bold girl with big dreams who had no issue declaring I'd one day change the world but also really wanted a blizzard from Dairy Queen. Where did that little girl go? Let me ask you the same question—when was the last time you named (without disclaimer or preface) what you wanted?

Throughout the Gospels we find Jesus asking a lot of questions. To the crowds and to individuals, we find He poses a total of 307 questions, and on more than one occasion He simply asks, "What do you want?" He famously asks Blind Bartimeus this question when the answer is obvious—Bartimeus wants to see. Jesus asks a paralyzed man lying beside the pool of Bethesda if he wants to be healed, when again, the answer is a clear-cut and resounding yes.

So why does He even ask when the answer is *so* obvious? Why does Jesus invite people to name what they want, and why, especially as women, do we struggle with withholding our requests? As I lay there that night, I was frightened at the realization that I had long ago abandoned the practice of naming what I wanted. And beyond this realization was the shocking truth that if Jesus stood in front of me and asked, "What do you want?" I would have no answer.

As a recovering perfectionist, working comes easier than asking, and performing for approval has typically been my

MO. On top of this internal drive to excel at all costs, I've faced thousands of small rejections and occasional failures that are a natural part of life. Somewhere between my childhood bunk bed and my cozy queen, it dawned on me: I'd lost something or simply settled for a new reality where I stopped naming and dreaming.

My story is different from yours, but I would guess that at the core, we have similar reasons why we abdicate naming our wants. Rejection. Embarrassment. Disappointment. To put it in Scriptural terms, our hope has been deferred one too many times, and we aren't sure how to get it back. We have wanted and been left wanting. We don't want to get let down again.

So we build walls of protection around our hearts, refuse to name what we actually want, and settle for assessing situations and determining the requests that will be appropriate for the current scenario or crowd. We occasionally go for dreams and even give voice to desires, but they are slivers of the truth, portions of the dream that we are willing to sacrifice on the altar of possible rejection. We dip our toes in the water, but we are too smart and too weary to actually dive deep and name what we want in full.

I think back to the woman with the issue of blood. Desperation compelled her to boldly go where she was forbidden, but she sought only to be physically healed, when Jesus knew there was more. More healing. More to want.

Jesus says in John 14:9, "Anyone who has seen me has seen the Father!" I think we have a generation of believers who agree with this concept mentally but haven't fully grasped it deep down. We are "good" with Jesus. His track record is easy to get behind, but when it comes to God as our Father, there are harder portions of Scripture to reconcile. Add that hurdle to the reality that many of us grew up with absent or checked-out fathers, and embracing God as Abba Father seems like a burden to overcome rather than an invitation to belong.

Abba, the Hebrew name for Father, was often on the lips of Jesus. When the disciples asked Him to teach them to pray, He began by explaining that they should start their prayers addressing God as their Father. This would have been mind-blowing for good Jewish boys, and it was blasphemous for religious leaders. In a culture where the name of God was not uttered for fear of taking His name in vain, the idea that God could be referred to in such a casual and relational term no doubt caused friction in the minds of those who grew up under strict rules but were now being drawn to this man of grace.

And Jesus didn't stop with the Lord's Prayer. Jesus talked about His Father and how the disciples could experience the Father through His own life over and over and over. It's as if He knew we'd need to revisit the identity of God as Abba multiple times before it would take root in our souls. I know in my own life, even though I have an amazing earthly father, I've still struggled to know God as Abba. As I mentioned earlier, duty and performance come more naturally than childlike faith or the holy act of simply being with God. It's hard to sit still and be loved by Him. I'd much rather earn His love, but that makes my relationship with God a transactional one, and Jesus already took care of all my debt.

Henri Nouwen writes, "The question is not 'How am I to find God?' but 'How am I to let myself be found by him?'"[1] Sometimes, like the woman with the issue of blood, God forces us to pause or stop so we can catch up to His love. And other times we encounter true childlike faith and are reminded that

1. Henri J. M. Nouwen, *The Return of the Prodigal Son* (New York: Doubleday, 1992), 106.

we've been living like an orphan settling for porridge when Abba has a feast readily available.

Discovering God as Father does not mean every whim and desire is automatically yours; it's a life-changing revelation that causes the frivolous wants to pale in comparison to the joy and security that come with being His. You, my friend, are not a slave or simply a servant. You are a child, a daughter, and when this identity takes root, it has the power to change everything.

This would be a great segue to tell you that Selah learned the hard but beautiful lesson that every prayer does not get a *yes*, but the truth is that a loving Father heard her sweet little prayer, and two weeks later, I found a young woman who attends our church in my office. I knew Jessica fairly well, but I didn't think she had ever met Selah. She called to ask if we could meet, and when she sat down, she explained that she had something strange to ask. She was engaged and in the midst of planning their wedding, and as she went to sleep two weeks prior, she had a dream about her upcoming wedding. She proceeded to tell me that in this dream, Selah, who she'd only seen from a distance and on my social media, was her flower girl.

Jessica explained that she wasn't planning on having flower girls, but after her dream, she really felt like Selah was supposed to walk down that aisle, and her fiancé had agreed! I was in complete shock. Jaw to the ground and mind blown, I sat in stunned silence, marveling that Selah was not going to be disappointed by the Father but instead would now have a monument to remember that He listens as we name our wants. Also, Selah was getting her *greatest dream ever*, and this made my mama heart overflow with gratitude to Him!

But you know what else is interesting about naming our wants and God answering them? I've found that His vantage point is so much higher and wiser that, sometimes, His answers come in packages, timing, or situations that are very different from the fantasies we create in our minds. So different, in fact, that if we aren't careful, we may actually wish we'd never voiced our want in the first place.

On the day of Jessica's wedding, I found myself in a conundrum as a young mother. The Saturday of the wedding was also Selah's first dance recital, so I knew it would be a long day for my spunky four-year-old. I had a plan, though, a solid plan: she'd knock our socks off as she danced in her clown costume that morning, we would jump in the car and drive an hour to the wedding site, she would take a nap during that drive, and all would be well. One small kink in the plan: the nap did not happen. So although the recital was a success, we pulled up to the gorgeous outdoor wedding venue lined with trees and hay bales as a frazzled mom with a tired four-year-old who was about to live out her dream on the verge of a meltdown.

We were ushered into the room where the bride and bridesmaids were getting ready, and Selah's eyes were as big as saucers at all the makeup and primping. I got her dressed in her cream lace dress that mimicked the bride's, and then the florist presented us with the Instagram-worthy flower crown that Selah was to wear. It was darling, and as I pinned it in her curls she smiled in the mirror with delight. Two minutes in to wearing this colorful flower crown though, and Selah began to squirm while exclaiming that her headpiece was itchy! I did my best to repin to minimize the itch, but when she didn't let up her complaints, I basically told her she needed to suck it up. Sometimes I'm awesome at being a mom. I was tired, and I forgot to mention this point: I was officiating the ceremony. So my margin was shrinking as I juggled my mom hat with my pastor hat, but like any good performer, I kept a smile plastered to my face as I gave her the side-eye to *stop complaining*.

We were then sent outside to take pictures before the ceremony started in a couple hours. The photographer had only snapped a couple photos when I realized my adorable daughter was standing stoic in the front of the bridal party, refusing to smile. Her arms were folded, her brow was creased, and she was clearly not having it even as the photographer did his best to try to coax a smile out of her. I whispered in a conspiratorial, all-knowing mother's way that we'd be right back.

I proceeded to yank Selah to the side and ask her what was wrong, and she said with the voice of a four-year-old who needed a nap that the flower crown was itchy and pictures were boring! I quickly saw that telling her to suck it up again was not going to work, so I pulled out all of my best parenting skills and started with bribery. I looked Selah in the eye and then in a singsong, happy voice asked if she knew what all happened at a wedding. When she shook her head, I raised my eyebrows and whispered, "At the end, there is cake. Lots of cake. So here is my deal: if you will smile, and take all of the pictures, and stop complaining about your flower crown, then I'm going to let you eat all the cake you want!" I don't know what I was thinking there, but desperate times and all of that. I definitely got her attention, and I could tell she was weighing what I was saying, but it didn't work. She sighed and said, "I just don't want to do it."

Okay, parenting tactic number two. This time I bent down so I was at eye level, and I did my best authoritative whisper: "Listen, young lady, you *will* go take pictures right now. You've agreed to be the flower girl and this is part of the job, so you need to change your attitude and go smile right now or there will be consequences." I stared her down. I thought I was getting through. But then I saw the quake of her chin and the tremble of her bottom lip. Next up, giant tears were forming in her big blue eyes, and before I could whisk her away, she was in a complete meltdown, ripping off that flower crown and throwing it on the ground as she began to sob.

Again, I looked at the photographer, bride, and all of the bridesmaids— who seemed semi-horrified—and lifted my finger as I said, "We're going to need a little more time." I wasn't sure what to do, but I picked up my baby (and the flower crown) and walked her over to the outdoor area where the chairs were set up for the ceremony. I rubbed her back and told her it was okay to cry. And I waited until she got it all out.

As she was doing that jagged breath thing that we all do after a great cry, I took a deep breath and asked the Father what He would have me do. He said in reply, *Remind her who she is.* I paused and looked around with fresh eyes, noticing the baby's breath draped over the wooden arch, the colorful wildflowers, the wooden doors that stood at the end of the aisle awaiting the big reveal, and then my girl. She was so pretty, and here she was crying in the moment that was supposed to be her greatest dream.

I took Selah by the hand and said, "Selah, look where we are!" She looked around, still gulping fresh air, and I began to point out all of the beautiful things I spotted. I asked her to point out what she thought was pretty, and she noticed things I hadn't—the tall trees and the cool stumps that lined the aisle. She was starting to enjoy this game, when I looked her in the eyes and said, "And who are you?" She looked at me puzzled, but I persisted. "Look at yourself! You've got your gorgeous dress, and the pretty flower crown—who are you?!" It took her a minute, but then in her sweet, childlike voice, she said, "I'm the flower girl."

"Say it again," I said.

"I'm the flower girl."

"Again."

"I'm the flower girl."

"Let's say it one more time!"

"I'm the flower girl!"

"Yes, you are! *You* are the flower girl. This is what you've been dreaming about. This is the prayer God answered for you. And listen, I know the flower crown is a little itchy and the pictures are not very exciting, but it's part of being a flower girl. But, Selah, the best part is coming! In just a little while, you are going to walk down this aisle right here. You are going to throw the petals, and everyone is going to be so proud of you. The best part is ahead."

She began to smile as she envisioned her moment, and when I said, "So what do you think? Can we go take a few pictures?" she scooped up that flower crown, slammed it on her head, and said, "Let's do this thing!"

I watched as she marched toward the photographer and let him know she was back and ready to smile, and as I stood under those tall trees, I heard the Father whisper to my heart, *She's just like you.*

I'm sorry, what?! *She's so much like you.*

And somehow internally I understood what He meant. More often than I'd like to admit I can get completely sidetracked and even consumed by the irritations of life. When I finally start to name what I want, I don't give God the freedom to answer in His best way, but I begin to create my own expectations. I think you might be like this too. We fantasize and play the what-if game in our minds, running various scenarios of what could be. Then we faceplant and find ourselves throwing tantrums when the dreams we concoct rarely meet reality. We are faced with itchy flower crowns and boring pictures.

Back and forth, our vision moves from blurry to clear, and it all hinges on our ability to remember who we are. One day we remember we are loved and worthy to name our innermost desires, but when prayers we've prayed begin to unfold, it's as if we contract amnesia, losing sight of our identity because we're focused on the uncomfortable responsibilities that come with being His kid. I'm certain you've faced these—the detours, the challenging people, the work in the trenches no one notices.

We question His ways.

I've got to embrace humility and serve alongside this person who annoys me?

It's an itchy flower crown.

I'm called to do the work that never gets any accolades, the emails and spreadsheets, the grocery shopping and car pools?

It's boring pictures.

And if we're not careful, we spend our days wasting time and standing stoic, rehashing the stuff we don't like instead of remembering who we are and the simple truth that there are beautiful moments, both now and on the horizon, connected to our identity as His daughter.

The woman with the issue of blood had her very own *greatest dream ever* experience where she went after what she wanted and received healing as she touched the hem of Jesus's garment, but then He stopped the crowd and went off script. Her greatest moment looked different than she expected because He knew she needed more. She needed Him to let her community know that she was clean and should be embraced with compassion after years of heartache and isolation. She needed emotional healing, and she needed to know that she wasn't alone but had a man, a Father, who would fight for her. And ultimately, she needed to be reminded of who she was—His daughter.

We don't know the rest of this woman's story, but I have a feeling she had her own itchy flower crown and boring picture moments, maybe even a meltdown or two, because most of life is lived out in the small details rather than earthshaking miracle moments. I hope she held on to the truth that at her core she was named daughter.

You may feel on the verge of your own meltdown today. It may feel like you are underappreciated, undervalued, and unseen. But there is a Father who knows your name. Instead of calling you Paige or Linda or Jennifer or Selah, He chooses to call you by a name so intimate, so personal, that you could never doubt His love for you. He calls you Daughter. It's a name that has power because it boasts of connection. It is a name that reminds all who listen that you belong. You have a Father—an Abba. He smiles on you, He stops crowds for you, and when you want to scream, He whispers an invitation to step away, take a deep breath, look around, and remember He knows your name.

CARVE YOUR NAME IN DIRT

The Woman Caught in Adultery

John 8:1–11

3

A Woman Caught

Another well-known gospel story of a woman whose name we don't know is the woman caught in adultery. Again, her identity, as we see it subtitled in most Bible translations, was wrapped up in one aspect of her life. One moment of sin. One moment of shame. She has a name, but the religious leaders were not interested that day in her true identity or the myriad of aspects that were tied to her life—her family or her dreams. They had another mission that day, a mission to try to trap Jesus as a hypocrite, and she was simply a pawn in their plan.

I'm going to call her "the woman caught in the middle," because although she was seized in the act of adultery, I don't want to define her that way. Her life was put on pause (hanging in this middle place) as she waited for what was next.

She was caught in someone else's scheme, caught in humiliation and scandal, caught under the stares of a glaring crowd, and caught in her own story. Her breath held, waiting to see if her very life would continue or be snuffed out in a moment. She also seemed to be caught unsure of what to do next. It's clear from the reading of the story that she was not given a moment to speak or defend herself. She was silenced. Silenced by the crowd and silenced by her shame.

Earlier I wrote about my friend Angel, and that in our ongoing conversations she eventually went silent, no longer returning our texts or phone calls. After a week of silence and conferring with Wendy, I reached out to Angel's sister, who lived in Tulsa as well. I remember standing in my kitchen, phone to my ear, as I explained our concern that we couldn't get ahold of Angel, and I still recall the ominous feeling in the pit of my stomach as I listened with clenched hands. I remember looking out the window as I heard the unbelievable words: Angel was silent because she was in the hospital. Her organs were failing, and the family had just left a conversation with the doctors where they explained Angel had a 10 to 20 percent chance of survival.

Everything around me stopped as my mind grappled to process this news. "Wait, what?! I was just there. How did this happen?!"

And the shock of her response, "Well, you know Angel is an alcoholic."

"Yeah . . . huh . . . what?" I literally couldn't form words as it became clear that her sister assumed I knew something that I had no idea about. Angel was an alcoholic. She had been for years. And her body could no longer keep up with the abuse. Her liver and her kidneys and her pancreas were shutting down. I don't remember much else about that conversation, except I asked if I could come see Angel. So I called Wendy, tears streaming down my face, hating the fact that I would be the one to tell her the news that our best friend was not just sick but dying.

We wept, and we wondered, how did we miss it?

Two days later, I found myself looking out another window, this time high above the clouds as I flew to Tulsa. I watched one of the most glorious sunrises, a mixture of pink and orange rising above a blue horizon. As I gazed on its beauty, reminding myself that His mercies are new each morning, I begged God to let my friend live. "I'm naming what I want, Jesus. I want you to wake her up. I want you to breathe life into her bones, and I want her to get the opportunity to raise her boys. I want my friend to live. We have more memories to make. More laughter and tears. More trips and more texts. More life."

Shoulders shaking, I curled up in that tiny seat, bargaining and proclaiming and pleading. Eventually my prayers were reduced to "Please, Jesus. Please."

Later that day, I found myself taking a deep breath and walking with Wendy into a Tulsa hospital, where we saw Angel's husband, Alan, sitting in the foyer, staring into the distance. After hugs, tears, and a long silence, Alan began to tell us the story. He explained how the alcohol addiction followed the postpartum depression and how they'd tried to handle it with doctor visits, counselors, and eventually multiple rehab stays. He told us that Angel promised him we knew and that we were trying to help or at least encourage her, and with tears pooled in his eyes he shared how this addiction, this sickness, had torn his heart in two. The story spanned almost a decade, and as we sat in that waiting area, people walking past with their own emergencies and heartache, I wept openly at all that was hidden, feeling my own heart shatter at the reality that my friend, my fun and fabulous friend, had lived a tug-of-war life for years. Suffocated by sickness and pain, silent under the oppression of shame, most days a shell of survival.

Addiction is a ruthless disease. It is persistent and loud, with no care for the destruction left in its wake. I don't pretend to really understand. I don't. Addiction has not been my battle, but I've walked alongside many friends who have tried to explain that even on the best of days, the voice, that voice of need and bargaining and false promises, is the loudest in the room. It's always there, taunting, coaxing, offering sweet relief from the current pain.

The voices we choose to listen to are powerful. Regardless of our version of tug-of-war—and you know we all have one—the loudest voice in the room or in our head can alter the life we thought possible. I think about the woman from Scripture caught in the middle, and what the noise must have been like that day. It's clear that the voices of these Pharisees were tinged with a vicious tone, hell-bent on finding some way to expose Jesus and His scandalous grace.

There was the voice of accusation, literally laying her sin out in the middle of the temple for all to see. More than likely she was stripped naked or barely covered, having been pulled from the act of adultery, and yet she alone is thrust in the dirt of wrongdoing. Where is the man she was with? The law clearly stated in Leviticus 20:10 and again in Deuteronomy 22:22 that *both* the man and woman caught in an adulterous relationship would be seen as guilty and subject to the punishment of stoning. Yet, notice the target of indictment and the injustice of the Pharisees' words as they raise their voices toward Jesus.

They said, "In the Law Moses commanded us to stone such women" (John 8:5 NIV). *Such women.* Did you see that? With two simple words, the religious leaders of the day, who were rarely questioned, not only bent Scripture to fit their agenda but also labeled, stereotyped, and created a narrative of this woman's life. She was "one of *them*," and with these damning words, her hope died a little more.

I'm sure there were voices of onlookers, religious men and women who came to the temple that day to learn but who now whispered to one another as they stopped and stared, transfixed by the wreckage like an unexpected accident on the side of the road.

And then what about the unspoken, yet well-known, voice of the law? John 8 makes it clear that this encounter occurred in the midst of the temple, right in the middle of Jesus teaching Scripture. He would have been teaching from the Torah, expounding on well-known verses that good Jewish boys memorized at a young age, and all in the room knew that disobedience to the voice of the law always required a swift punishment. This sin, this scandalous sin of sleeping with a married man, carried a sentence not of shame or censure but death. A life . . . her life, forever over.

External voices clamoring to be heard were undoubtedly roaring in her ears, and yet I believe that just as boisterous were the internal voices sneering and jeering inside the mind of this woman caught in the middle. The voice that said, "Stupid girl . . ." followed by a personal lashing of why she'd said yes. The voice of what might have been, saying good-bye to future hopes while trying to brace for what was sure to follow. The frantic voice, wondering if there was any way out, and the voice of internal desperation, "Please, God. Please."

Even in ordinary moments, I often have three to four voices competing for my attention. And when I'm in seasons of change or wondering if I'm seen, the voices seem to multiply. Take any internal tug-of-war situation: mommy guilt, loneliness though surrounded by people, a desire for peace when you can't please everyone, internal wrestling when your beliefs are changing, or facing your own version of injustice. The voices can be deafening. Shame. Hope. Despair. What-if. Comparison. It's voice after voice and breath after breath, desperate for help to decipher what is right and true. I know I'm there often. You probably are too.

Everyone waited with bated breath for Jesus's response to the Pharisees. I shout from the sidelines of Scripture, "Put them in their place, Jesus!" Rather than answer them, John

8:6 says, "Jesus stooped down and wrote in the dust with his finger."

He slowed the pace. He didn't take the bait. He was silent, but His very presence spoke volumes. He bent down. He came close. He got dirty as He wrote in the dust.

No one knows what Jesus wrote in the dust that day. Debate and educated guesses fly around, but John doesn't let us know what He wrote, and I have to believe that it's because what mattered that day, what shifted the atmosphere, was not the words written but the *man* who wrote them. When His words, etched in the ground, entered the scene, everything changed.

We live in a world where women are frantically searching for a voice or words to make sense of life and of the feelings of being caught in the middle. We share Instagram quotes like they are going out of style; we lift up witty one-liners; and we immerse ourselves in the latest self-help books, hoping if we just wash our face or learn how to be a #girlboss that maybe, just maybe, we will know we are seen and heard. And here's the thing: quotes, wise teachers, and books are not a problem (I mean, you are reading a book at this very moment), but they are more voices clamoring for attention when so often we don't need to go looking far and wide but rather slow the pace, come close, exhale that breath we've been holding, and discover Jesus is speaking.

I've had countless people over the years ask me how to hear His voice. Is it audible? Does it leave a funny feeling in your gut? Is it profound and earth-shattering? Rarely, sometimes, and could be, but mostly what I've found to be true about the voice of Jesus, which I see on full display in this story, is the simple truth that His voice is for you. John 1:17 (NIV) says, "For the law was given through Moses; grace and truth came through Jesus Christ."

His voice is clear. His voice brings peace. His voice drips with love. His words are often simple while turning your world upside down in the best way. And when you hear His voice for yourself, not a secondhand version, but His voice speaking directly to your heart, it carries a weight that connects with your soul. His simple words may sound sweet to others, but when it is for you and to you, it's a fresh breath and an invitation to exhale. Everything is going to be okay even when it's not okay.

The voice of Jesus is the ultimate game changer. In this story, for instance, He flipped the script and invited any Pharisee who had never had lust or sin in the hidden confines of his own heart to go ahead and throw the first stone. Jesus shifted the focus from the outward sin of a vulnerable woman to the inward sins of proud and conniving men. And one by one they dropped their stones, if not their pride, and slipped away.

Don't be surprised when the voice of Jesus causes you to see a situation completely differently. He sees each of us from the perspective of Creator and Redeemer, so when we try to implement behavior modification, He will instead point to the heart issues—insecurities or wrong beliefs. His voice is always for us, inviting us to shift our understanding of just how good He really is, unveiling truth while wrapping it in grace.

I relearned the truth that the voice of Jesus is often unexpected yet always good the day I went to visit Angel in the Tulsa hospital. Words fail me as I try to describe the heaviness and grief that grew that day as we went up the elevator and encountered Angel's sisters, her brother, and her parents. Some were numb, some were believing in a miracle, some were angry, and some were just so very sad. Alan thought it would be best if everyone cleared the room and allowed Wendy and me to have some time alone to sit with our friend. She was no longer awake, but we sat on either side of her and grabbed her hands—the three of us, together again, facing far more than freshman homesickness like that first day together.

Sitting in that sterile room and staring at my friend, I said a few words that felt inadequate and hollow, so I settled for silence, listening to the sound of machines, when I had what I'd call a God moment. It was as if I could see Jesus sitting in the bed with Angel. He was gazing at her, gently stroking her hair back from her forehead, and there was an overwhelming sense of peace in my heart and also in that room. I immediately remembered all of the prayers and petitions from my plane ride, and I thought, *Are you going to heal her?!* And that's when I heard Him whisper to my heart, *Do you want her healed and free, or do you want her back?*

And I knew. Maybe because of the conversation I just had with Alan or because I was seeing her in His presence, I'm not exactly sure, because God moments aren't always a three-step process, but I knew that having her back was not the same as her being healed and free. Her healing and freedom would only occur in His tangible presence, and I had to give up my definition of what healing was to look like for her. So I breathed deep and exhaled as I told Him, "I want her to be free." And with those words I knew. I knew I was saying good-bye.

Jesus has His own good-bye moment with the woman caught in the middle. After all the Pharisees left the temple, one by one, shrinking away to lick their wounds and make more plans, we find Jesus alone with this woman. He asked her, "'Where are your accusers? Didn't even one of them condemn you?' 'No, Lord,' she said. And Jesus said, 'Neither do I. Go and sin no more'" (John 8:10–11).

And with those life-giving words she was moved from being caught in sin and injustice to a place where a future was possible. Jesus allowed her to exhale as He offered forgiveness as well as a command to go! No longer stuck in the middle, she was reminded that her identity and her name were not associated with "such women," but rather she was a woman destined for a life of freedom and purpose.

Jesus came to set people free. He set people free as He walked the earth, and He continues to free people today—from sin, from addiction, from injustice, and from despair. Some days we find ourselves like the woman caught in the middle, gasping for air and looking for a way out toward freedom, and other days, we end up like the Pharisees, trying so desperately to hold on to what we've known that we can distort true freedom to meet our agenda. But when we are able to stop long enough to gaze up at Jesus, we gain His perspective. We see others through His eyes. We understand situations through His truth, not ours.

As I think back to that God moment in Angel's room and the tender way Jesus flipped the script to my own desperate prayers, I realize that surrendering to His ways of healing and freedom will always be better than getting what I want. He gave me peace when I lifted my eyes and slowed my pace, remembering that He was there. And yet, it still hurts. I miss my fun and fabulous friend. I miss her laugh and the twinkle she got in her eyes when she had an idea that no doubt would stretch me, her straight-laced friend. And I still have questions. So many questions. I wonder about what kind of a mom she would have been and why an all-powerful God didn't heal her at some point in her addiction journey. I question and inhale. I surrender and exhale. Over and over and over.

And you know, the longer I walk with Jesus, the more I'm reminded that life is made of middle moments. Moments when voices are loud and moments when the silence is deafening, with just a beep of a machine in the background. Moments when we feel caught and embarrassed, looking to see if someone will rescue us. Life is made of middle moments where we feel adrift and exposed, moments when all we know to do is to cry out, "Please, Jesus. Please." But there is a promise in the middle. When we lift up our eyes in the midst of the chaos, the focus changes from our shame and confusion to the man writing in the dust of our lives. He is there, and you are seen.

4

An Advocate Defends

One part of my job that is the messiest, but also the most rewarding, is working alongside other amazing women at a place called the New Legacy Home for Women. We call it New Legacy Home because we believe God is giving each woman who walks through our doors a chance to start a new story, and our goal is to give them tools over the course of fifteen months that will allow them to succeed once they leave our safety and supervision. Walking alongside women coming out of incarceration, prostitution, abuse, and rehab can be extremely difficult, as we often are navigating hidden landmines in their hearts, but like I said, it's also become the delight of my life to watch as God provides amazing miracles and unfathomable heart transformations for these women.

I've always been drawn to justice issues. Quick to sound the alarm or raise awareness for needs, I love feeling like I'm a part of setting the world straight and seeing people pulled from places of darkness into God's goodness. There is something about advocating, using my voice on behalf of those silenced or shining a light on the truth of a situation, that always leaves me feeling like I'm in step with God. And I know I'm not unique in this pull toward sounding alarms and helping the unseen. As believers, becoming advocates is natural because it's in our DNA. Jesus Himself was the strongest advocate, and we watch this aspect of His character shine in the story of the woman caught in the middle.

Recently, I walked into the New Legacy Home at 7:00 a.m., ready to do my weekly devotional with the women, when I was greeted with a new face smiling shyly underneath heavy bangs. I introduced myself and found out she'd arrived just the day before, fresh off the street and desperate for change. I'll call her Whytney.

Whytney had been prostituting in order to survive but then had found the courage to knock on our door and ask for help. She was a little jumpy, weepy, and hunched over with shame, yet also wide-eyed with a sliver of hope. I watched her sneaking glances around the home and at the various women, who I knew would soon become her sisters, silently questioning whether this was her new reality or just a dream sure to be snatched away.

My story is far different from Whytney's, but catching her eyes underneath those bangs reminded me of a time when the weight of shame left me feeling small and questioning my purpose and future. As I mentioned, I met Jesus as a child and found myself in church every time the doors were opened. And as much as I sought after Jesus's love, I was still a teenage girl who secretly wanted a boyfriend most of junior high and into high school. The boys tended to orbit around my best friends though, and I was often the third wheel, wondering what was wrong with me. Well-meaning people would quip that I must not have a date because I intimidated the boys. I was never sure how to take this comment.

At the age of sixteen, I finally had someone show interest in me, and since he was four years older and in college (West Point, no less), I finally understood those previous comments made to me. I deduced that I did, in fact, intimidate boys because I was just too mature. With a flick of my ponytail and a wave of my hand, I thought, *So long, boys. I'm off to date a man.* A college man, in fact.

I dated this boy-man for a little over a year and quickly decided I was in love. We only went on two actual dates because he had no money, and we were separated for most of that year, writing letters back and forth from New York to Texas, but he made me laugh and he was masterful at creating mixtapes. (Is there anything more powerful for inducing teenage love than the perfect song list?)

It was a relatively harmless relationship in hindsight, but over the course of that year, I chose him and his preferences over myself and who I really was over and over again. At just sixteen, I was figuring out who I was. I was experiencing my own version of namelessness, trying on different personalities for size, and at that time, many happened to be influenced by my boyfriend. Although I was a leader up until that point, known as someone who could be counted on, I found myself desperate to be accepted—so desperate, in fact, that I settled for my name to be *his girlfriend* and abdicated previous names of *leader* and *justice seeker* for *confused follower*.

He cared little about his faith, so I set mine on a shelf too. His humor was sarcastic and often at the cost of the most vulnerable person in the room, so I silenced my internal compass after his jokes and pretended to giggle, all the while grieving internally that I was now complicit with an unfair one-liner. I morphed myself to fit what I believed he wanted, and when he broke up with me, I not only lost a boyfriend but realized I had also lost much of myself along the way. I was devastated, heartbroken, and furious with myself. And in that place of grief, shame creeped in and began to feed me a buffet of lies.

Teenage me, who was voted Most Likely to Succeed, berated myself at night and questioned whether I was still worthy of God's love and the big plans I had in my heart. If I could so easily discard core beliefs just to gain favor with one boy-man, how was I to know I wouldn't trade in my faith in the future when faced with a new person to please? And if my secret desire and calling from God was to be a female preacher, then how could I reconcile my desire to call people into His love with the reality that maybe His love wasn't even enough for me? How could His love be enough if I was willing to so quickly abandon it and cross the physical and sexual boundaries I'd previously set up to protect my heart, if not my body, for the first boy I dated? And was it even possible to actually be me and still catch someone's eye? Was loving a true version of myself even possible? Or would I always have to morph myself to fit whoever showed interest next?

I asked question after question. I desperately wanted to regain my confidence and passion for Jesus, but because so much of my faith had been wrapped up in behavior and perfectionism, I honestly began to believe that I must have forfeited His purposes when I chose to walk away from His best. It's one thing to understand with our minds that Jesus wants to be our advocate and extends His love toward us, but it is another thing entirely to take Jesus's hand and allow Him to advocate for us and silence the shame.

It was during this season of questions that my dad asked me to travel to Guatemala with him. I was often his international travel buddy when he spoke at pastors' conferences around the globe. I had been to Guatemala once before and marveled at the people, colors, and beauty to such a degree that I chose to extend my study of Spanish when I returned home, hoping to find myself back in that country in the future. This trip should have been an easy yes, but I was hesitant to go, as the shame and lies that I was a disappointment wrapped tighter around my mind. I said yes anyways, but I told my dad that I wanted to basically hide in the background and let him do the real ministry. He didn't really respond to my request, but with a little side hug and his all-knowing nod, he made it clear that he just wanted to spend some time with me.

Remember how Zack Morris would do a time-out on *Saved by the Bell* to make a point? I'm going to do that here because I want to talk about Jesus before I finish this story. *Time-out.*

I've started to study the idea of Jesus as our advocate because I believe this word best describes His actions in John 8 as He interacted with the woman caught in the middle. An advocate is someone who pleads or defends another in public. This definition is clearly what Jesus does in this narrative, but it's also what He does for us personally. Upon the cross of Calvary, Jesus took our sin, bore our shame, and made us right before the Father. He is our safe haven and strong defender.

First John 2:1–2 (ESV, emphasis added) reads, "My little children, I am writing these things to you so that you may not sin. But if anyone does sin, we have an *advocate* with the Father, Jesus Christ the righteous. He is the propitiation for our sins, and not for ours only but also for the sins of the whole world."

The word translated as *advocate* in this portion of Scripture is the Greek word *parakletos. Advocate* (in English) paints a picture of someone standing up and speaking on behalf of someone else, but in its fullness, *parakletos* is less about someone defending and more about someone who comes close and walks alongside. It is this word, *parakletos*, that Jesus uses in John 14 when He tells the disciples that the Father will send a

Helper who will walk with them forever. That Helper (*para-kletos*) is the Holy Spirit. The Holy Spirit doesn't get nearly as much airtime as I think He should, so I want to shine a spotlight on the fact that He is alive today in the lives of believers as our advocate and helper. He walks with us day in and day out, and He desires to come close.

If I have learned anything about being an advocate in my time working at New Legacy, it's that speaking out on behalf of our women is the easy part. I can give a presentation or raise funds or even speak in front of a judge about the worth I see in each of our ladies without a hitch. But the messy and harder-to-define parts of being an advocate are found in the moments when the Lord directs me or one of our staff to come close and ask a question to one of the residents that peels back layers of hurt or shame. It's complicated, like trying to get a tangled knot out of a delicate chain, and I've learned that the unseen and unglamorous moments are what really mark someone as an advocate. Being a true advocate is shown in the day-by-day walk, from the time a woman enters our doors to the day she graduates, as we continue to believe the best and choose to love even when shame or fear causes one of our ladies to lash out with hurtful words. It's in the times when we come close, and it's in the days and hours of living life side by side that trust and hope are restored.

And the same is true of the Holy Spirit and Jesus as our advocate. Yes, He will and does speak out on our behalf, but His nature as advocate is to come close and walk with us side by side, day in and day out, as the *parakletos*. It's fewer grand gestures and more quiet whispers. It's that persistent knocking and insistence that we expose hurts or shame to His healing light. It's the unseen moments with Him holding our hand that actually bridge the gap and cause us to feel seen and known.

For the woman caught in the middle, it was Jesus bending down to her level and writing in the dust that mixed with her tears. He stayed close to her, and when all the accusers stepped away, He stepped closer and called her to righteousness and purity as He named her *free* and admonished her to sin no more. He was her advocate, and He wants to be ours, but there is often a hesitation on our part.

When He draws near, ready to peel back layers of pain, do we welcome His presence, or do we hide, stiff-arm, and ignore His voice?

Years ago, the Holy Spirit exposed something in my heart about this issue. We were having a big family dinner at my parents' home. My sister was engaged to an awesome man who had a four-year-old daughter, and we were in full wedding-planning mode. After dinner, everyone got up from the table and began to clear the dishes and move toward the kitchen. There was laughter in the kitchen as my sisters and mom talked about weddings gone wrong, and I hurried toward the dining room to whisk away the final remnants of our feast. As I rounded the corner, I stopped in my tracks and observed the cutest conversation between my dad and soon-to-be little niece. My dad was bent over so he could be at eye level with her, and as I stood in the doorway, I heard him say, "I want you to know I love you and I'm so glad you are going to be part of my family." Now, my dad is not one to be overly expressive with his emotions, so I was well aware that I was hovering over a special moment, and I choked up simply witnessing his tender words to this precious little girl.

But imagine my surprise as my niece cocked her head to the side, lifted her hands upward like perhaps she was a bunny, and without missing a beat, let out three loud barks. "Ruff, ruff, ruff, I'm a little dog!" she proclaimed. I wasn't sure whether to laugh or step in and admonish this sweet girl that she was missing the point of this heartfelt moment, but I remained still as I watched my dad stand up and with a small shake of his head and grin on his lips, he gently reached out his hand, patted her head, and said, "Okay . . . good little doggy."

I went to pick up the remaining silverware when the Holy Spirit nudged my heart with this thought: *You do that to me all the time.* I stopped, glanced side to side, and then whispered back in my mind, *I'm sorry, what?!*

You do that to me all the time.

And as conversations tend to go with me and the Lord, I understood what He meant with that one phrase. I realized that the barks of my niece were actually the defense mechanisms of a four-year-old girl who at a young age had already experienced deep rejection. As much as our family was trying to get to know her, she was trying to discern whether we could be trusted, or if this was another opportunity for heartbreak. She might have only been four, but she already had a defense to protect her heart. When my dad came close, she pulled away the best way she knew how.

And then God said, *You do that to me all the time.* And He was right. My defense mechanisms are a bit different from barking like a dog, but when God tries to come close or invite me to a place of vulnerability in the light of His love, my defenses rise up and I push Him away. For example, when I found myself late at night questioning God about the boy-man, there were moments when I felt Him trying to come close and heal the wounds in my heart, rather than answer the questions of my mind. But I wasn't ready to receive that love. I felt unworthy, and I was scared of what would be exposed deep down if I actually got vulnerable with God. So I kept His love at bay, trying to convince myself that "I'll be fine!"

I do this now as a forty-something-year-old woman too. Just last week, a friend made a passive-aggressive remark that felt like a personal dig. I found myself later that day driving in my car, tears welling up, and I felt Jesus the Advocate come close and ask what was beneath the pain of that remark. I knew He was trying to peel back layers and shine His love into that wounded corner of my heart, but instead of leaning in to a place of vulnerability, I chose to bark. I turned up the volume of the radio, willfully chose to think about the next thing on my to-do list, and literally said out loud, "I'm too busy. It's not a big deal; I need to move on." Don't we all do that with the Lord sometimes? We ignore the promptings, the tears, the heart beating just a little faster, and we convince ourselves that we are either fine or busy or something in-between.

I wish I'd remember there is a better way, because on the occasions I silence my bark, often in a moment of worship or when walking in nature, the outside world quiets down long enough for me to see Jesus bent over and looking me squarely in the eyes. He is my *advocate*. He loves me, and He's so glad I'm part of His family.

Unfortunately, I think most of us believe that walking with Him is limited to small, extraordinary moments—a handful of miraculous stories we tell from time to time. We believe that the day in and day out parts of our life are inconsequential to an omnipotent God, and we just need to press on and get the day done. We may say small prayers, but at our core, we keep firmly in control and walled off from true vulnerability with Him. When God speaks to us through our occasional Bible reading, we shrug it off as a coincidence, and when God prompts friends who check in to see if we're really okay or if we should talk to someone after or during hard seasons, we choose to tell half-truths, giving those friends just enough of the story so it feels as though we're being candid, when in reality, we keep the real pain away from their loving eyes.

If a four-year-old knows how to keep a loving grandfather at bay, how much more skilled am I as a forty-four-year-old at keeping my heavenly Father at arm's length? We settle for Jesus as an occasional spokesperson when He wants to be our groom, living life as One who is close and walks hand in hand with us each and every day.

Life with Jesus is not a formula to crack but a walk-it-out relationship where we get to know Him as the advocate or *parakletos*. In fact, the Greek word *parakletos* is only used by John in his writings. We find it used four times in the gospel he wrote, as well as once in his letters, and I can't help but wonder if this disciple who calls himself "the one Jesus loved" had a true revelation of Jesus as our advocate simply because he was willing to allow himself to be loved.

Can we allow Jesus to love us today?

I mentioned going to Guatemala with my dad after my breakup with the boy-man, and during that trip, I had a moment that showed me how being loved by Jesus starts by seeing ourselves as He sees us.

We landed in Guatemala to a beautiful welcome, and after hugs and a meal of chicken, black beans, rice, and fried plantains, the pastor of the church where we ministered said, "Paige, I hope you will speak to us too while you are here!" I did my best to graciously decline, explaining that my dad was the speaker and I was simply there to spend time with him and see my Guatemalan friends. He must have thought I was just trying to be modest, because this pastor was insistent in his request that I address his congregation, and his invitation continued until my dad finally said, "I'm sure Paige would be happy to share a few words."

I was not happy with my dad, but in order to not offend, I agreed to share briefly the next night, and spent the next twenty-four hours in a mental shame spiral, reminding myself of all the reasons I had no right to be on a stage exhorting the people at this church. I rehearsed the many ways I'd walked away from God in the last year in pursuit of the boy-man. I hadn't slept with him, but I was tempted to, and in my mind, the heart issues and abandonment of my values were just as damning as the actions I could have taken. Although just two years earlier I was confident that I was called to preach, I now believed that dream was lost because I'd followed a man instead of Jesus.

Bottom line, I was a seventeen-year-old girl who talked a big game and still wore a winning smile, but internally I felt unworthy, unclean, and fearful that to step on that stage would be the epitome of living like a Pharisee—claiming one thing with my lips but knowing my heart and life had been far from the truth I was now proclaiming. I was a fraud, and I believed that as soon as I stepped on that stage, my shame would be on display for all to clearly see.

But I'd agreed to speak, and I genuinely loved these people, so with quaking knees I went up the creaking steps and did my best to share a few words I knew to be true. I don't remember the content of my words, but I remember talking as quickly as possible so I could duck down from the stage and return to the anonymity of my plastic blue chair as my father got up to preach the real sermon that night. I felt better, having gotten it over with, and although I knew in my mind that God forgave me and was offering a fresh start, I couldn't seem to shake how angry I was with myself. I didn't know how to forgive myself, let alone trust that I wouldn't derail my life again in pursuit of something that appeared greener or flashier.

Fighting with yourself and clearly seeing the angel and demon sitting on your two shoulders is a maddening tug-of-war, something I experienced as I sat in that plastic chair surrounded by people who were listening to what my father had to say. As they listened, I wrestled and questioned, begging God to help me sort out which Paige would lead my life.

When the service was over, there was a long line of fervent people all clamoring for my dad to pray for them, asking for healing or blessing or wisdom from God. I knew my dad would stay as long as it took to pray for each and every person in that line, and although I was encouraged to pray for people as well, I declined and moved to the side to stay out of the way.

I had been there for quite a while, watching as people wept with upheld arms to God, when I felt a tap on my shoulder. I looked up to see Anna, my favorite translator. She asked me to come over to where a hunched-over Guatemalan woman wrapped in a colorful huipil, the traditional clothing of Guatemalans, was standing. As I walked over, I got a better look at this woman, who reached out her wrinkly hands for mine, and I realized that she had likely lived longer than almost anyone else in this room. Her hair was streaked with gray, a cane was at her side, and the lines on her face were deep and too numerous to count. But as I took her hands and looked into her eyes, the smile that overtook her face was breathtaking, and a feeling of peace was so tangible that I squeezed tight, thinking I needed to hold her paper-thin hands for a long time.

She began speaking rapidly to Anna, nodding her head in my direction with such force and animation that I knew she had something profound to say. My head swiveled from Anna to the woman like I was watching a tennis match as Anna tried to gain a full understanding of what this woman wanted me to know. Anna's eyes moved from surprise to purpose in an instant, and she smiled at the woman, said a few words, and then turned her attention to me.

"Paige, this dear woman has walked with the Lord for many, many years, and she wants you to know about something that happened to her tonight. She says that tonight was just like any other church service for her, and she was looking forward to hearing your father speak. But as soon as you stepped on the stage, it was as if heaven and earth collided, and she saw two things. First, it was as if a spotlight from heaven was shining down on you, and it enveloped you and moved with you with each step you took. Second, as you stood under that spotlight, your clothes began to change, and you were no longer wearing this black skirt and blue shirt you have on right now, but they transformed before her eyes into the most beautiful dress she's ever seen."

I glanced over at this woman, my heart hammering and my eyes wide, only to meet her eyes that overflowed with such a fierce but compassionate love that my breath caught in my throat. Anna continued, "She says this dress sparkled and was radiant, the most beautiful garment she's ever seen. She was mesmerized and overtaken as she watched you up on stage, and then she heard a voice. And the voice said these simple words: 'Go tell her that this is how I see her.' And so she is being obedient to the Lord.

"But, Paige"—Anna took a breath and looked again at this old woman, who nodded at her while still looking intently at me—"she says that she wants to add to those words and tell you if He sees you like this, it's time for you to believe Him and begin to see yourself the same way. You are spotless. You are radiant. You live under the light of His love."

As I'm sure you can imagine, I was completely undone and openly wept in the arms of Anna and this woman. I never got her name, but under the loving gaze and prophetic words of this nameless woman, I was forever changed. Imprinted on my heart from that day forward was the truth that God walks with me and shines His loving light on me not because of my behavior and perfection but because being my advocate and the *parakletos* is His very nature.

Friend, you live under the light of His love too. Regardless of the sin, shame, or lies of your past, Jesus desperately wants to be your advocate. He sees you not in the dust of today but in the glory of your future. And when He comes close, ready to heal or whisper, you have a decision to make. Will you believe His voice of love and open your life to the work He wants to do in the recesses of your heart? Or will you choose to bark?

Day in and day out, Jesus advocates for us all. Even when we choose to hide or ignore or pretend that we are too busy, He is still there. His presence is not fickle. His desire to come close and simply be with you is not capricious or erratic. He is constant, and He is your advocate.

MAKE
A NAME
FOR
YOURSELF

The Woman Bent Over
with a Crippling Spirit

Luke 13:10–17

5

A Woman Suffers

She is less well-known than other nameless women (I'm looking at you, woman at the well), but one of my favorite accounts of an anonymous woman is found in Luke 13. It's a short but powerful encounter between Jesus and a woman who was bent over from a debilitating disease or tormenting spirit. The verses are few, yet I always marvel in awe as I read of the faith and tenacity of this tiny woman who shows up in an unlikely place, the synagogue.

> One Sabbath day as Jesus was teaching in a synagogue, he saw a woman who had been crippled by an evil spirit. She had been bent double for eighteen years and was unable to stand up straight. When Jesus saw her, he called her over and said, "Dear woman, you are healed of your sickness!" Then he touched her, and instantly she could stand straight. How she praised God!
>
> Luke 13:10–13

I've always been drawn to this story because when I picture this woman bent over, I see in my mind's eye my Mema during the last decade of her life. Mema had rheumatoid arthritis, and as her years progressed, her knuckles swelled and her back slowly curved inward to such a degree that she often made jokes about her shrinking stature. My Mema was a strong yet petite woman who always had her raven hair fixed just so. She visited her hairdresser every other week to get those luscious locks colored, teased, and shellacked into an unmovable yet shiny helmet that I sometimes surreptitiously patted to see if it was as stiff as I imagined (it was). She went from being known as a fierce matriarch to a sweet grandma who could be found most days reading her Bible or racing down the hallways of the local retirement home in her motorized wheelchair that we lovingly named "the Jazzy."

I noticed the glances of pity, the quick double takes directed at her swollen hands anytime we encountered strangers. We would roll into Schlotzsky's for our monthly lunches, and without fail, servers would direct questions my way while looking over the top of Mema's head, even though she was right there, rolled up to the counter in her Jazzy. As servers dismissed her presence, I remember thinking, *If you only knew.*

If you only knew that this woman now confined to a wheelchair once walked with resolve as she found herself a widow at age thirty-five, with four grieving children whom she raised into amazing adults, you might direct your questions her way. If you only knew that this slight woman riddled with disease decided to keep the family farm and oversaw 1,280 acres of dryland cotton all on her own, you'd probably actually look her in the eyes. If you only knew that this woman just buried her second husband after watching him decline with dementia, you might slow down and listen. If you only knew that these gnarled hands taught me to bake an unforgettable apple cake and wrote out prayer requests daily on a small scroll that hung in her hallway, evoking both awe and fear in the hearts of all her grandkids as they secretly looked to see who made the list, you might see her the way I do.

You might actually see her.

But they didn't know, so the pimply-faced cashier would quickly ask what kind of chips she wanted with her turkey sandwich and hurry along to the next customer in line.

Why is it that as a culture, we (I'm including myself in this indictment) focus on the glittery and grand? Young. Famous. Popular. Impressive. Loud. Talented. We take notice of who or what everyone else is clamoring after, yet so often we miss out on the small and deep.

If we only knew.

This is why I love this story. It's a short excerpt about a small woman bent over who comes face-to-face with Jesus, a man who does in fact know.

I read this story and think of the well-known Shakespeare quote, "Though she be but little, she is fierce."[1]

Why is she fierce? First, take a closer look at her situation. When we meet this unnamed woman in Luke 13, we realize that she would be very easy to look over, as Scripture says she literally could not straighten her spine. Scholars debate the root of her illness, but regardless of the underlying cause, the truth remains that she was in pain and had been so for eighteen years! Eugene Peterson's paraphrase in *The Message* describes her as being "so twisted and bent over with arthritis that she couldn't even look up" (Luke 13:11). Can you imagine? Eighteen years of not being able to look up at the sky or hug your child or lengthen your body as you sleep. Eighteen years of staring at the ground when you'd prefer to look deeply into people's eyes. Eighteen years of being overlooked, dismissed,

---

1. William Shakespeare, *A Midsummer Night's Dream* (New York: Signet Classic, 1998), 52.

and pitied when you have opinions about life and wisdom to share.

What we see and where we focus profoundly affects our lives. You've likely heard the adage that we become what we behold, and I believe there is much truth to that statement. When seasons of illness, diminishment, heartache, and disappointment loom large, it is a fight to hold on to hope. Why? Because what we see and what we focus on have a way of informing our thoughts, feelings, and eventually beliefs.

If Satan can't fill your heart with unbelief, he will spend his time getting you bent over so all you can see is your issue. Many of us are bent over, focused on the rejection of the past or our anxiety about the future. This woman was literally bent over with illness and had been so for eighteen years. I can't imagine the battles she faced in her mind and heart, and yet I call her fierce because even though her outward reality was still crippled, her internal posture was one of standing with great faith. She won the battle over her focus because when she had every right to stay home and weep, she chose instead to show up and worship.

Showing up and simply doing the next right thing is a fight, but it is also a victory. It feels small, and yet in the kingdom of God, simple acts of faithfulness are the very thing that capture the attention of a loving God.

I don't think it is a coincidence that following the story of this woman bent over, we find Jesus sharing two parables about His upside-down kingdom. Look at His words following her healing:

> Then Jesus said, "What is the Kingdom of God like? How can I illustrate it? It is like a *tiny* mustard seed that a man planted in a garden; it grows and becomes a tree, and the birds make nests in its branches." He also asked, "What else is the Kingdom of

God like? It is like the yeast a woman used in making bread. Even though she put only a *little* yeast in three measures of flour, it permeated every part of the dough."

Luke 13:18–21, emphasis added

Do not underestimate the power of the small. The mustard seed. The yeast. This woman. All appear to be small in the economy of our world, and yet in the kingdom of God they have the potential to grow, expand, and infuse life.

We know this. In our minds we know small can be good. We applaud simple acts of kindness. We teach our children about contentment. We post on Instagram about slowing down and being present. We say we believe a small life can be a good life.

So why is it when I talk with women and they get brutally honest, most feel like they are missing out? Why are we looking over our shoulders, feeling as though we didn't get the text about the best party in town? Why are we scrolling, scrolling, scrolling, imagining what our homes and bodies and family could look like if they were just a little more shiny, a little more popular, a little more beautiful? Why are we spending ridiculous amounts of money on our homes and vacations, our bodies, and our children's sports? We say we know small is powerful, but we sure are treating our ordinary lives as if they are an ailment to cure rather than an opportunity to embrace.

Ladies, I'm preaching to the choir here. I understand the tension of wanting to embrace small while craving the elusive spotlight. For too many years, I've dreamed of bright stages and gazed longingly at lives I deem successful, trying to figure out where I'm falling short. I've analyzed and wondered what I should add or do in the hopes of getting one step closer to an enticing image that seems just out of reach.

I want to be "used" by God, and for too many years I defined that as actions that are visible and make headlines rather than embracing the opportunities smack-dab in the middle of my real and small life. I've been bent over thinking about what-ifs when right nows slip by in my peripheral vision.

A few years ago, I traveled to Mumbai, India, with a small team on a mission to minister to women throughout that colorful land. It was my fifth trip to this vibrant nation, and although my husband often describes India as a land that assaults the senses, I had come to love the way life teemed with fervor in this foreign place. The sharp smells of unknown spices, the sounds of horns honking and children laughing, and the excitement bordering on terror at what surprising sights we might stumble upon after each turn delighted and lit up my soul. With each successive trip, I fell more and more in love with the people of India. They were resilient, funny, and desperately hungry for God. So with an overflowing heart and jet-lagged brain, my feet hit the ground with purpose and desire—I was there to infuse hope as I pointed women to a loving Jesus who saw them in the midst of the color and spice.

This trip was a whirlwind of activity and service opportunities. My team visited schools in the midst of slums where tiny children dressed in light blue gingham uniforms confidently shared their ABCs. We spoke in churches, orphanages, and a beautiful home that served as a safe haven for women rescued from human trafficking. We listened, prayed, sang, and gave a lot of hugs. It was stacking up to be another trip for the books.

On the second-to-last day of the trip, I looked at our itinerary and saw that we had two final meetings scheduled with women. The first was in a middle-class home where the women spoke fluent English and met weekly over chai and biscuits (cookies) to learn about the Lord. I was invited to speak, and as I entered the apartment, I remember thinking that I almost felt at home, as if I was in a small group back in Texas. The women were at ease with one another, laughing at inside jokes and complimenting each other on the delicious snacks they'd brought that day. A few of the children not yet in school played in the background, and as I talked to the women, the Lord clearly prompted me to speak on worry and His promise for peace even when anxiety wants to suffocate all hope.

As I spoke to these modern young mothers, they leaned in and I felt them drink in every word I shared. We laughed at our similarities, and then tears began to form as the women shared about the worries that plague their minds late at night. It was a holy morning—filled with hot chai, loving prayers, and the tangible presence of God. I didn't want to leave.

But the schedule was set, and we had a long way to drive to another part of the city. I remember as we dodged traffic, swaying in the minivan, my friend began to share that we were traveling into a poorer part of the city, and instead of meeting in a home, we would be in a concrete room that was occasionally rented out by a church in the area. The pastor and his wife who were hosting the event welcomed us and warned that word had spread, and they expected the room to quickly fill to capacity. Sure enough, the room overflowed to such a degree that women started sitting in the next room, listening through the doorway, while others stood outside, peering through the small barred openings that served as windows.

Worship was vibrant with a small keyboard and loud voices reverberating off the tin roof. These women stood shoulder to shoulder, arms lifted to heaven and tears streaming down most faces. I stood with my back touching the cool concrete, very aware I was in another holy room with women God desperately loves. He prompted me to share on worry again, and I smiled at the realization that though material differences were obvious between this group and the other, the women's questions and fears were similar regardless of location. Through a translator these beautiful women ate up every word I shared, and because no one could move, individual prayer and hugs were changed to a sweeping blessing I declared over God's daughters.

I got back to my hotel late that night, high on adrenaline and yearning for sleep. My phone rang as I was dozing off, and my missionary friend asked if I could squeeze in one more ministry moment on our final day. She acted kind of funny about the invitation, explaining that the rest of the team could not accompany me, as some of the ladies who would be in attendance needed security or privacy. I immediately said yes and fell asleep, thanking God for the day filled with chai, saris, and love.

The next day I found myself traveling alone with my missionary friend to a part of the city that had clean streets lined with pricey cars. It was quieter, calmer, and the air somehow felt cleaner. As I entered a shiny apartment, I was struck by the women in the room. They were young, *gorgeous*, and at ease with one another. They laughed, poured chai, found comfortable seats on pillows and chairs, and settled in for what appeared to be their weekly small group session. They went around the circle, sharing their names and brief bios. Most appeared to be actresses, models, or somehow connected to Bollywood (side note: if you've never seen a Bollywood movie, please go do yourself a favor and watch one ASAP). I reconnected with a vibrant and powerful young female pastor who I'd met a few years earlier and discovered that she and her husband had started a church focused on the "up and in" rather than the "down and out." She was discipling these young women who were impacting India's culture.

The night went well. I spoke on worry *again*, and we had plenty of time for individual prayer, encouragement, and laughter. It too was a holy moment—a place where young women scrutinized by society found a safe space for vulnerability and friendship. It was beautiful.

I traveled home the next day, reflecting on those three different holy moments. The settings and situations were vastly different, and yet the women were so similar—struggling with the same questions and all hungry for more of God. I knew I'd be asked about my trip and was excited to share about these amazing women from vastly different worlds.

But here's where I messed up. On my second night home, wide awake at 4:00 a.m. with jet lag, I moved to the couch and began to scroll on my phone. Instagram is my mindless go-to, and as I scrolled, I decided to find the girls I'd met on that final night. It wasn't hard to stumble upon each profile. They were public figures in India, most with a blue check next to their name, but I was shocked and then secretly thrilled to see that these girls weren't just in the industry but *famous* in the industry. I gasped as I clicked on one profile, discovering that one young woman who sat across from me makeup-free and crying in vulnerability had three million Instagram followers—*three million!* And then with the next click I found out the young woman who kept the conversation going and spoke truth to many was a former Miss India! *Miss India?!* And on and on I went, sucked down a rabbit hole of discovery and ego boosting.

Guess what? The next time someone asked me about my trip, the narrative that I'd previously held was drastically different. No longer was I talking about those three holy moments. Instead I was talking about how God had granted *me* the opportunity to minister to a room full of beautiful, famous women. I have no doubt that I exaggerated just how much God had used me and how I was now connected to their lives. Ugh! I cringe to think about this now.

Thankfully, God convicted and exposed my behavior one Sunday morning as I prepared to share this story with a roomful of people. Sitting in my office, I felt undone as God asked,

Why do you want to be connected to what the world deems famous? I've called you to love people, so what is driving you to share about some when I love them all?

Here is what I discovered in my own life—this drive to be connected to "cultural shiny" goes back to the root issue of feeling my value increases when I'm associated with something or someone who receives the approval of others. I don't think I'm alone. We want to be seen, to be noticed. And when our small lives feel dismissed, unseen, or even belittled by the standards of Instagram or current culture, we sometimes try to attach ourselves to anything shiny in the hopes we might get a little peripheral light shining our way too.

It's a distraction from God's best that goes back to the beginning of time. It's why thousands of people flocked to Jesus when He was multiplying bread and walking on water but only a handful remained when He was mocked and slapped on His way to the cross. There is a certain kind of security and fleeting happiness when we find ourselves squarely in the middle of the thing everyone else is clamoring after, and yet, how often are we missing out on what God is doing or blessing because our focus is locked on what stands tall rather than what bows low?

I'm so thankful that I know a Jesus who graciously corrects me when my focus gets off His best. He confronts me when I start to act like a Pharisee, clawing after what makes me seem great in the eyes of others, and He meets me with His healing truth when I focus on my issue, bent over in shame and despair.

What I see in this woman bent over is similar to what I felt in the holy moments located in three different rooms across India. We can show up without a glow up. We are invited every day to come as we are, and Jesus will meet us there.

There is a sort of freedom in embracing our smallness, because in God's upside-down kingdom, we find His loving gaze when we stop pretending we are grand and instead own our ordinary. I love the way Tish Harrison Warren says this: "We come to know God when our ability to perform, to measure up, to achieve, fails us."[2] There is power in coming to Jesus when we have nothing to give or show off. This woman bent over is faithful to show up. She does not wait for deliverance or healing, but she comes in her brokenness to worship.

Charles Spurgeon reflects on her story with these words:

> She could not stand upright, but she could come as she was— bent and infirm as she was. I rejoice in my Master's way of healing people, for he comes to them where they are. He does not propose to them that if they will do somewhat he will do the rest, but he begins and ends. He bids them approach him as they are, and does not ask them to mend or prepare.[3]

What if the focus of our lives was less on getting near what the world deems great and more on simply getting into His presence? Might we find those feelings of internal worth and the genuine light our soul longs for? Our nameless woman definitely experienced this light. "How she praised God!" (Luke 13:13). Being caught under the loving gaze of Jesus leads to transformation.

2. Tish Harrison Warren, *Prayer in the Night* (Downers Grove: InterVarsity Press, 2021), 96.

3. Charles Spurgeon, "The Lifting Up of the Bowed Down," July 14, 1878, *Metropolitan Tabernacle Pulpit* 24:421–32, The Spurgeon Center for Biblical Preaching at Midwestern Seminary, https://www.spurgeon.org/resource-library/sermons/the -lifting-up-of-the-bowed-down/#flipbook/.

6

A Shepherd Releases

When I turned eighteen, I traded in the flatlands of West Texas for the rolling hills of Oklahoma. I chose a university where I knew only one person, and I was both ecstatic and nervous about the possibility of all that lay ahead. I was still occasionally talking to the boy-man, as he would write letters dripping with apologies, but with the crossing of the state line, I felt the impact of his words dim and became more aware than ever that now was the chance to cut destructive ties from the past and create a new future, if not a new me.

Some of the best advice my wise mama gave me came about a week before I left home. We were sitting on my bed packing up a few items when she said, "You know what's going to be great about your college experience? No one knows who you are, so you can be who you've always wanted to be."

Those words landed deep like an anchor in my heart, and I started asking myself, *Who do I want to be?* I would later discover that this one question guided many decisions as I navigated this new world of late nights, cute upperclassmen, and forever friends (like Wendy and Angel).

Having received yet another letter from the boy-man, I sat at my tiny dorm room desk, responding with a simple note asking that he please not write again. I was clear-eyed about the life I wanted, and I knew that life could not include a toxic relationship. As I sealed the envelope, I told the Lord that I was now taking a break from boys. This felt like a big sacrifice, but I wanted to focus on becoming the kind of woman who laughed often, embraced challenges, and had late-night conversations with friends. Boys would have to wait.

A couple months into my new college life, I was walking with Wendy along a winding sidewalk when out of the clear night sky I heard a booming voice call out, "Baylor?!" The voice was loud. It was male. It seemed close, and it definitely grabbed our attention. We stopped in our tracks, and then we both glanced at my sweatshirt emblazoned with the word *Baylor*. So I guess that cry was directed at me?! Suddenly we saw a dark-haired, determined young man bound over to us, rambling with nervous energy that he had almost gone to Baylor. His enthusiasm was contagious, and the conversation wandered to commonalities about Texas and knowing a handful of the same people.

As he walked away, Wendy said, "Wow! He clearly likes you."

"No he doesn't," I declared. "He was just excited to see something that reminded him of home." Wendy smirked and shook her head at my oblivion. It was clear. The Baylor! guy definitely liked me.

My denial and protestation slowly began to wane over the following weeks as the Baylor! guy, who was named Josh, continued to randomly show up in my life. I kid you not, every day I would report to my friends about the Josh sighting of the day. Although I had not seen him once in the two months prior to our meeting, I now seemed to run into him constantly. At a concert, in the cafeteria, and even near my classes, which was particularly odd, as I was a communications major and he belonged to the school of business. There he was, over and over and over again. I may have initially used the word *stalker* with my friends, but slowly my view of him changed, and I realized that with each encounter or conversation, I didn't feel angst like in drama-fueled relationships of the past but rather saw myself as the girl I wanted to be.

I am happy to report that I wound up marrying the Baylor! guy, and that Baylor sweatshirt now resides in a shadow box on our bedroom wall. It reminds me of that whimsical conversation under the stars, but it also reminds me that when I was trying to figure out who I wanted to be, there was someone who saw me, and once he did, he couldn't unsee me.

My husband is not Jesus, but I feel like the quality in his life of seeing and pursuing reflects the Jesus who occupies his heart. I mentioned in the previous chapter how Jesus knows and sees the bent over woman when she could easily have been overlooked, but He does more than just see. He sees, He heals, and then He protects.

Look at what happens in the synagogue after Jesus heals the woman bent over:

> But the leader in charge of the synagogue was indignant that Jesus had healed her on the Sabbath day. "There are six days of the week for working," he said to the crowd. "Come on those days to be healed, not on the Sabbath."
>
> But the Lord replied, "You hypocrites! Each of you works on the Sabbath day! Don't you untie your ox or your donkey from its stall on the Sabbath and lead it out for water? This dear woman, a daughter of Abraham, has been held in bondage

by Satan for eighteen years. Isn't it right that she be released, even on the Sabbath?"

Luke 13:14–16

I love the way Jesus uses His voice to cover and protect this marginalized woman. She has just experienced the best day of her life and is standing straight for the first time in eighteen years. Can you imagine this?! She is standing up. Straight. No longer relegated to looking at dusty feet, but now witnessing through tears the smiles and shock of those she has known for years. She immediately begins to praise Jesus, and don't you know her heart was absolutely overflowing with gratitude, joy, and utter awe. For the first time in her life, she is the center of wonder. People are not pitying her but marveling instead. And in that moment, her moment, the leader of the synagogue fires an accusation her way. He acknowledges she is healed but points out that this marvelous work should have been done on a different day. For years I believed that this passage had the leader hurling accusations toward Jesus, but when you read it again, you see that this religious leader is maligning Jesus by slinging blame at this woman. She is the easier mark. So he shames her and condemns her, saying she should have come on a different day.

When this leader takes a vicious swipe at a vulnerable woman, Jesus steps into the ring ready to go to blows. You can see Him turn His attention from this woman to this proud man, ready for the challenge ahead. He holds nothing back as He declares the religious leaders hypocrites who care more about their livestock than the well-being of the people they serve. Jesus is just as fierce in His protection as He is lavish in His healing.

He is a true shepherd and demonstrates the qualities of a good shepherd as He takes her under His wing, standing at guard, ready to attack illness and shame alike. The ancient world regularly used images of a shepherd to describe the authority and care exercised by leaders. It's littered throughout ancient writings: Babylonian, Egyptian, and Jewish alike.[1] God describes Himself as a shepherd in both the Old and New Testaments.

There are beautiful writings found in Ezekiel 34, where God declares, "I myself will search and find my sheep. I will be like a shepherd looking for his scattered flock. I will find my sheep and rescue them from all the places where they were scattered on that dark and cloudy day" (vv.11–12).

I also love Isaiah 40:10–11 (NIV), where the prophet writes, "See, the Sovereign LORD comes with power, and he rules with a mighty arm. See, his reward is with him, and his recompense accompanies him. He tends his flock like a shepherd: He gathers the lambs in his arms and carries them close to his heart; he gently leads those that have young."

And perhaps the most well-known and loved Scripture about God as shepherd is Psalm 23, where David writes a song of praise reminding himself and us of just how good God really is. He starts his melody with a short but utterly powerful statement: "The LORD is my shepherd; I have all that I need."

Because of *who* the Lord is, all desire and need is covered. It's profound when you stop to think about it, and yet we live in constant want, perhaps because we do not truly believe the first part of these ancient words.

The Lord *is* my shepherd. Notice that these words are in present tense. David is not reflecting on God's protection in the past but rather is mindful of who God is today. I have no doubt that many of us would love to live free of envy and certain of providential care, but the conversations I overhear and the

1. John H. Walton and Craig S. Keener, eds., *NRSV Cultural Backgrounds Study Bible* (Grand Rapids: Zondervan, 2019), 899.

messages I read on Facebook make it clear that most days we are questioning God's hand rather than trusting His heart. How do we actually start to believe that He is our shepherd today?

I love what Dr. Tony Evans says: "In order for Him to be your Shepherd, you must first recognize yourself as a sheep."[2] In all my research on sheep, the reoccurring adjective used to describe this small but stubborn creature is the word *dumb*. I read numerous accounts explaining that sheep are directionally challenged and have been known to literally follow the sheep in front of them right off the side of a cliff. I also discovered that sheep often die from eating too much good food[3] or gulping so much water that they wind up toppling into rivers because their woolen coats become so dense that they lose their balance. This picture of a dimwitted sheep with a craving for excess, face submerged in cool waters, unaware as it tries to drink more and more and more, gives new meaning to the line "He leads me beside still waters" (Psalm 23:2 NRSV). Good shepherds know that instead of excess and more, sheep need calm and fresh. It is for the sake of their survival that shepherds seek out still waters, so that when sheep inevitably drink too much and fall into the water, they can be pulled back to safety rather than lost downstream.

Dying from falling off cliffs or being swept away because you just wanted a drink does sound kind of dumb to me, and yet I was stopped in my tracks as I read Margaret Feinberg's conversation with an actual shepherdess in her book *Scouting the Divine*. When Feinberg mentions this idea that sheep are dumb, the shepherdess looks at her clearly and says, "They are not dumb; they're defenseless."[4]

2. Tony Evans, *The Power of God's Names* (Eugene: Harvest House, 2014), 117.
3. Margaret Feinberg, *Scouting the Divine: My Search for God in Wine, Wool, and Wild Honey* (Grand Rapids: Zondervan, 2009), 53.
4. Feinberg, 55.

Defenseless. Directionally impaired. Seeking and consuming more and more to the point of our detriment. As much as I hate to admit it, that does sound like us. We are sheep. Prey who are open to the enemy and quick to follow the masses, how many of us secretly ask ourselves, *How did I get here?* We clamor and consume. We say yes when we should say no, taking yet another drink out of life—more stuff, more likes, more commitments, and more praise—but after a while, the weight of our pursuits topples us over and we find ourselves calling out for help as we float down the rushing river of anxiety and overwhelm.

What would happen if we admitted our weakness? What if we embraced our smallness and got honest about our need for limitations? Could we really follow a *good shepherd*? Could still waters and upright living be a normal part of our lives?

When I was a little girl, my grandfather decided to diversify his cotton farm and start raising cattle. I loved driving out to the pasture with him as he fed his herd, and it was obvious that he was smitten with this new way of utilizing the land. A few years into his cattle venture, the idea was thrown around that someone should enter the local 4-H stock show. It turned out that someone would be me. Now, I was a city girl through and through. Yes, I enjoyed going out to the pasture and watching the cattle, but up until this point I usually stayed inside my grandfather's truck, whereas now I was expected to walk and feed and bathe two enormous smelly animals. It was a different level of up close and personal.

I was given two steers to raise that would be shown after a year of growth. I lovingly named the black beauty Sugar Baby, and I decided on Sky Walker for the restless red one. I was excited about my new yellow cowgirl boots, and my mom made me colorful bows for the stock shows in hopes it would garner the judges' attention. But a year is a long time, and as the weeks progressed, my excitement waned. I realized that

93

walking one-thousand-pound steers was a lot of work compared to my previous extracurricular activity of dance class.
I complained. I cried. I often called my grandfather's ranch
hand and asked him to feed the beasts. I dreaded long walks in
the hot sun, and I hated how dirty and stinky I would be after
giving one of them a bath. My grandfather was counting on
me so I stuck it out, and I even won the showmanship award
(I think it was the bow). It was a good lesson for a growing
girl, but looking back, I'm more aware than ever that I was not
a good animal owner to those two steers.

In the specific story of the woman healed from being bent
over, we see Jesus use an agrarian illustration in His censure of
the religious leaders. He doesn't mention sheep specifically, but
He does speak to the heart of a good leader and animal owner.
He explains that any responsible animal owner will make sure
his animals have access to water on the Sabbath. This was a
given in this culture, and all those in the synagogue that day
would have undoubtedly thought of their own livestock, if not
the idea of what it means to be a good shepherd.

Good shepherds set aside their desires for the welfare of their
flock. Unfortunately, this woman and many people today have
not experienced what it means to be shepherded by a good
leader. K. J. Ramsey writes, "I believe so many of us don't really
sense and experience that the Lord is *our* Shepherd because we
have rarely been shepherded by people who stand with us in the
dirt of our distress."[5] This was the case for the bent over woman,
abandoned in both her distress and now in her healing, yet look
at how Jesus is quick to bring correction to this corrupt leader.

Jesus censures this man for neglecting the care of this woman
who considered the synagogue her place of worship. He calls
him out, and then Jesus communicates two more things that

5. K. J. Ramsey, *The Lord Is My Courage: Stepping Through the Shadows of Fear Toward the Voice of Love* (Grand Rapids: Zondervan, 2022), 17.

beautifully demonstrate for all watching what it actually means to be a good shepherd.

First, He gives this woman a name. It's not her given name—we don't read about a Mary or Lydia—but He extends even greater dignity to this woman as He connects her life to their forefather. He calls her "a daughter of Abraham" (Luke 13:16), which reminds all in attendance that this woman is valuable. She is part of the family and should be treated with respect.

John 10:3–4 says, "He calls his own sheep by name and leads them out . . . and they follow him because they know his voice." This statement in Scripture is not hyperbole. Shepherds did name their sheep, and those sheep would come running when they heard their name called.

Our good shepherd knows your name, and He delights in reminding you and me that we are connected to His bigger story of grace. Like this woman who now stands tall, you too are a daughter of Abraham. You have been grafted into the family of God and now stand as an heir with promises from on high (see Galatians 3:29).

The second attribute of a good shepherd that Jesus demonstrates in this narrative, and specifically as He rebukes the synagogue leader, is that He exposes the ultimate enemy. Yes, Jesus is frustrated with this unjust human leader, but He is equally if not more so intent on exposing the primary enemy who has harassed this dear woman for long enough. He says, "This dear woman, a daughter of Abraham, *has been held in bondage by Satan for eighteen years.* Isn't it right that she be released, even on the Sabbath?" (Luke 13:16, emphasis added).

He calls Satan out as He sets this woman free. She was not simply sick, but she was bound by the enemy, and He is making it clear that as the *good shepherd*, He is taking back His authority. It's no coincidence that as Jesus speaks of Himself as the good shepherd in John 10, there too He exposes the lies and plans of the enemy: "The thief's purpose is to steal and kill and destroy. My purpose is to give them a rich and satisfying life" (v. 10).

And how is He going to do this?

Just keep reading: "I am the good shepherd. The good shepherd sacrifices his life for the sheep" (John 10:11).

It's a drop-the-mic moment in Scripture. Let it sink in. Jesus *is* the *good shepherd*.

He came to bring life. Rich and satisfying life.

He sacrificed His life for you. For your freedom. For your healing.

He sacrificed His life so that, similar to when I headed to college, you might have the freedom to ask yourself, *Who do I want to be? Who does God say that I am?* You don't have to cross state lines to change who you are: you merely look toward the shepherd, believe you belong in His family, and begin to stand up. Am I making it sound too easy? Yes. Moving from bent over to standing tall is usually a process, but it is possible. It is!

To place an exclamation point on this story of the woman bent over, I think we should take note of the fact that the number eighteen is mentioned twice in the retelling. Anytime specific details such as numbers are included (especially if they are mentioned more than once), they are present to point to another layer of truth.

Guess what the number eighteen means in Hebrew numerology?[6] It means *life*! And specifically, life after bondage.[7]

6. Hebrew numerology can sound weird, but it stems from the fact that Hebrew numbers are traditionally written using letters from the Hebrew alphabet. So numbers can spell words, and words can add up to numerical values. There are agreed-upon meanings for numbers one through twenty, which is why you may have heard about the significance of three, seven, or twelve. Here too is an example of a number containing meaning that speaks to the moment. One word of caution: be careful not to jump to conclusions or assign meaning every time a number is used in Scripture.

7. "Meaning of Numbers in the Bible: The Number 18," Biblestudy.org, accessed March 13, 2023, https://www.biblestudy.org/bibleref/meaning-of-numbers-in-bible/18.html.

Joshua led the Israelites for eighteen years in the wilderness before they entered the promised land, and this woman is freed from physical illness after eighteen years, entering into her own promised land as she now stands tall.

Luke includes these details to speak to readers like you and me centuries later. When the shepherd, a *good shepherd*, begins to lead your life, freedom is on the horizon! Some of you may have experienced the pain of being led by a harsh or abusive shepherd. Like the woman bent over, you may have received wounds or been shamed by someone who should have protected you. I am so sorry. I know a little about the pain this can cause, and I know it creates barriers in our hearts to believing good shepherds exist. My prayer for you today is that this story would serve as a reminder that Jesus wants to be your shepherd, and He *is* the good shepherd. He heals and He also protects. He does not care what day you show up, He simply asks that you do.

A GOOD NAME DESIRED ABOVE RICHES

The Widow with Two Mites

Mark 12:41–44 & Luke 21:1–4

7

A Woman Sacrifices

If you've spent much time in churches across the world, you've likely heard about the widow with two mites. Her recorded story is short—only four verses in two different gospels (Mark and Luke)—yet her sacrificial gift of offering something small when she had none to spare is a story that continues to resonate. This brief but powerful narrative is a fan favorite for pastors wanting to emphasize the virtue of giving finances and time, and perhaps that is the very reason why so many people have ignored this woman's story. In all transparency, I was tempted to skip over this unnamed woman, thinking surely there wasn't much more to unearth from her shining example, but as I began to study, I realized that her life caught Jesus's attention for good reason and continues to speak to us today.

There are two obvious things we know about this woman: she was a widow and she was poor. If you grew up staring at Sunday school flannelgraphs or have a PhD in Beth Moore Bible studies, you likely know that widows were considered the most vulnerable of Jewish society during Jesus's time on earth. As mentioned earlier, in this patriarchal world, a woman's worth and provision were connected to the men in her family. Jewish women had very few rights of their own. They could not testify in court or engage in commerce. Women were expected to stay within the confines of their homes, and when any woman was brave enough to venture outside the walls of her abode, it was silently demanded that she be accompanied by a male member of her family. Most women were illiterate, and although they were allowed into the temple, they could not go beyond the women's court.

These descriptions may catch you off guard, as we already encountered women alone on the streets or in the temple running into Jesus in our previous chapters, but that's okay. Be astonished and stunned! These stories *were* shocking to the people of Jesus's day. The Pharisees were distressed, and the people were intrigued, because Jesus, the popular rabbi with the ragtag disciples, not only tolerated but welcomed women as He taught and traveled.

Add the lack of a husband or any male relative to these restrictions placed on all women, and you begin to understand the desperation and fear that many widows undoubtedly felt. Yet the Bible is littered with stories of bold and brave widows. We read about the widow of Zarephath in 1 Kings 17, where Elijah had the audacity to ask for a slice of bread even though this widow was making her final crusty loaf before she and her son starved to death (good news: God showed up through this beseeching prophet and provided a miracle of more than enough). We also read about two widows who are center stage in the book of Ruth. Readers cheered for Naomi and Ruth as they gleaned leftovers from fields (the primary method of survival for widows) and sought a kinsman redeemer to ease the burden and isolation of their lives as widows.

Jesus Himself used images of widows in some of His parables, going against the grain of culture to remind His listeners
that though these women may be on the bottom rung of society's pecking order, in the kingdom of God they were near the
top. In fact, God's plan was that these vulnerable women were
to be protected and cared for by the community. In Deuteronomy 24, He institutes the gleaning laws so that widows will
have food available, and I love the words of Psalm 68:5 (NRSV):
"Father of orphans and protector of widows is God in his holy
habitation." God wanted to be known as the protector of these
precious women, and His command to care for widows was
not limited to the Old Testament. James, the brother of Jesus,
writes these words to believers of the early church, and they
ring true for us today as well: "Pure and genuine religion in
the sight of God the Father means caring for orphans and
widows in their distress and refusing to let the world corrupt
you" (James 1:27).

When we take this into consideration, we shouldn't be surprised that we find Jesus watching a widow, a poor widow,
bring a small amount of money to the treasury in the temple.
Depending on the translation, her offering may be described
as two copper coins, two mites, or a farthing. My research
shows that one of these coins was 1/128 of a denarius.[1] A denarius was a Roman silver coin considered standard pay for
a full day's work. So if we do a little math, we can deduce that
she is in essence giving the amount a man would be paid for
ten minutes of work.[2] Scripture says this miniscule amount
is "all she had to live on" (Mark 12:44 NRSV). The injustice
of her situation reeks. Didn't God command the community to provide for these widows? How does the amount a

1. John H. Walton and Craig S. Keener, eds., *NRSV Cultural Backgrounds Study
Bible* (Grand Rapids: Zondervan, 2019), 1732.
2. *NRSV Cultural Backgrounds Study Bible*, 1732.

man makes in ten minutes equate to enough for a woman's livelihood?

Another striking piece of information about this encounter is that it occurred during the final week of Jesus's life as He resolutely made His way to Calvary. He entered the city on a donkey to a feverish pitch of praise, and He found Himself assailed with constant criticisms and cunning questions as the Pharisees hoped to trap Jesus and add to their case. The air was electric with gossip and miracles alike. And Jesus, He was not there to play. He knew His time was short, and He was focused on the things that mattered most.

Jesus was intent on exposing the lines between dark and light. His words about the widow's gift were a teaching moment for the disciples and were in sharp contrast to the scene Jesus made the day before. If you flip back in your Bible to the previous chapters of Mark 11 and Luke 19, we read about Jesus raging in this *exact location* as He flipped tables and shouted about the purpose and purity of the temple. And here He is now, hours later, praising this widow as memories of His righteous anger and raised voice still echoed in the minds of the masses.

Jesus was fed up with His Father's house being used to line the pockets of men while widows struggled to survive. He had spent the last three years trying to demonstrate the kingdom way, a way of humility and honor, a way of love lived out, a way of lifting the lowly and exposing the false. His time was coming to an end, and I imagine Jesus taking another deep breath as it dawned on Him that so many still didn't get it. So He sat down and began to watch as people brought their offerings to the treasury, and there in the midst of so much pride was this widow dropping two coins into the box. *Clink. Clink.*

As Jesus watched this impoverished woman bring a small gift with a desperately pure heart, I can't help but wonder if the Father orchestrated this moment, at this specific time, as an encouragement to His Son. *Look, my Son, the work and your words have not been in vain. There are those in Israel who understand what it means to surrender, to trust.* This simple moment was a reminder to an exhausted rabbi that Calvary was necessary for people, people like this widow. I see Jesus take another deep breath as the widow's presence and sacrifice blows over His weary mind like a gentle breeze. And He calls out to His disciples for one more lesson, a simple but profound lesson: *be like her.*

Sometimes it is the elementary and straightforward statements in charged settings that leave the greatest impact on our lives. I can't help but connect this story to one of my own from way back in 2006. My husband and I were leading a guided tour through Israel in July of that year and had assembled a team of twenty-six people ranging in age from early twenties to early eighties—a genuinely diverse team filled with precious people eager to walk where Jesus had once traversed. We were scheduled to leave on July 14, and if you do a quick Google search, you will discover that on July 12, 2006, a war with Lebanon broke out in the northern part of Israel. I'll never forget how my phone rang nonstop on the thirteenth as I was fielding calls and trying to decide whether we should still take this team to the Holy Land.

My contacts in Israel assured me it was a small conflict and we would be in zero danger. I read everything I could on the situation and ultimately collapsed on my couch, a ball of nerves, and simply asked Jesus, "What should I do?" I lay on my olive-green couch for almost an hour, ignoring the rings of my phone and begging God for an answer. I've heard it said once before that the best way to hear from God is to get neutral about the decision you need to make. So I laid down my preferences as well as the fear, and finally found myself neutral, declaring I was ready to go or stay, whatever He said, we would do. When my mind had quieted and I knew He could be trusted, I sensed a peace from above and a whisper to my heart that we should still go. I called all twenty-six team members and explained what our contacts told us and let them know they should only go if they too had peace about the journey. Within an hour, all but one decided to get on the plane and fly into a military conflict.

Within our first hour of landing in Israel, we found ourselves standing outside a kibbutz and receiving a quick but efficient training on how best to take cover if we happened to hear a high-pitched siren in the air. The serious but kind guide explained that these sirens would only sound the alarm if a missile was actually incoming (there would be no preliminary warning), and therefore we had approximately forty-five seconds to seek shelter before the incoming missile would strike. I remember someone raising their hand and asking, "I'm sorry, did you say forty-five *seconds*?!" Yes. We looked at one another with wide eyes and shocked grins. What had we gotten ourselves into?

The next day as we toured the northern part of Israel, there was an eerie quiet. The streets were desolate, and stops that I knew were typically hot tourist locations were empty of all buses but one (ours). We spoke with several locals who had a weariness in their eyes, explaining that living on high alert was not abnormal, so they would carry on with a determination that I found both inspiring and exhausting. After visiting a few sights in the north, our guide felt confident that we could take our planned boat ride on the Sea of Galilee. The sky was clear, and there was a small hope that peace would soon resume. Having traveled to Israel once before, I knew how special a boat ride on the sea where Jesus calmed a raging storm would be for my team, so I eagerly agreed and ushered our team onto a wooden boat designed to look and feel similar to a boat from Jesus's day.

The first thirty minutes of our boat ride were glorious. Someone led a short devotional about Jesus calming the waves and walking on this very water. We took Communion together as the boat drifted further into the middle of the sea, and I remember sighing as I thanked the Father for giving us the nudge to still come, a reminder that even in conflict much like the stormy sea, He was with us. This set-aside time on the water felt like a promise, and to add to the ambiance, the weather was gorgeous! It was a bright day with calm waves, birds were in the air, and I could feel the joy rising in our team. We encouraged everyone to spread out over the expanse of the boat to enjoy the scenery and quietly reflect or worship.

We turned on music, choosing "Shout to the Lord," and I watched my team raise their hands in praise. As I write these words today, remembering this moment, I realize Darlene Zschech's voice is forever etched in my memory, because as she belted out her words of praise in that song, I heard a faint, high-pitched noise emanating from the shore. I strained my ear toward the noise and then searched the faces for our guide. Right as I made eye contact, he gave me a curt nod, and then I watched as he whispered furiously to the boat driver while simultaneously reaching for a knob that I realized was increasing the volume of our music so that "Shout to the Lord" all but drowned out the sound of an incoming missile.

The boat began to turn and pick up speed as it headed back toward land. Although several of my precious friends were oblivious to what was happening (they were really worshiping along with Darlene), we eventually got everyone's attention, and our calm guide began to explain what was happening. We were in fact hearing missile sirens from Tiberias. There were reports of rockets incoming, and we had already missed the forty-five second window of grace; therefore, upon landing we were to *run* as fast as humanly possible and crouch by a rock wall while we waited for our bus to return so we could *get out of there!*

As you can imagine, news that we were now in danger caused quite the commotion. I saw fear in eyes and spouses whispering to one another as each person attempted to grapple with this surprising reality. For the most part the team remained calm and stoic as we jetted toward land, and it was as we sped forward that my husband came to my side and reminded me that as the leaders of this team, we were responsible to make sure everyone got safely back onto our bus. I think his actual words were, "Paige, I know we want to run, but we can't leave anyone behind." He was right. We were young, strong, and fast, but others on our team were not so agile. We looked around the boat, our eyes landing on the three women with gray hair and canes in hand. We divided them up—Josh would help the small woman with the bad hip, another strong man would help a woman I'll call Barbara, who was feisty but slow, and I would walk alongside the oldest on our team, a widow in her eighties named Wanda Teal. Wanda was in the best health of the three, so I felt good about my assignment, and I went to stand next to her so we could make a break for it as soon as possible.

The boat skidded into the dock, and before it was secured, I watched as the young and spry on our team leapt from the stern and began to sprint toward the haven of the rock wall. The sirens were still ringing their alarm, and they pierced my ears as anxiety threatened to overtake my heart and mind. I watched as others walked quickly and gasped as my husband hoisted his assigned partner into his arms so he could make better time. The crowd was thinning, as one by one the team made their way to the wall, and I realized with another gulp of fear that Wanda and I would be the last to arrive safely. We were walking at a decent pace, but I sensed no frenzy or compulsion to pick up speed from her. So with my best leader-of-the-team voice, I squeaked through my fear, "Ms. Wanda, do you think we could go a little faster? I really do think it's important we get to that wall as quickly as possible."

And then, to my utter shock and dismay, she slowed down. She slowed down! We were still walking, but her steps seemed to disconnect from my frenzied pace and instead began to move with a new sense of resolve. Wanda looked me in the eyes as we crept toward that rock wall, and with her West Texas drawl she said, "Darlin', the Lord promised me long ago that I would one day get to see the walls of Jerusalem. I've waited over eighty years to see that sight, and it's not on our itinerary for another two days . . . so I figure I've got at least another forty-eight hours before He takes me out." She chuckled and looked my way with a gleam in her eyes. I was speechless.

I'm happy to report we made it to the rock wall, and eventually we were back on the bus driving out of Tiberias like we were in a scene from *The Fast and the Furious*. As the bus jostled, making hairpin turns at lightning speed, the inside of the bus teemed with tears and talk. This was before social media or cheap international phone calls, so most of the team huddled together rehashing what had just happened and whether our lives were really in danger. I sat alone, away from the chatter, staring out the window as buildings and trees raced by in a flurry. I was stunned and my mind raced, not at the possibility of bombs but because of the words of a wise widow. Her wisecrack had cracked open something deep within my heart, and I sat there thinking, *How was Wanda so at peace?*

How did she *know* His promise was certain? How was it that a widow who had waited over eighty years now treated God's whispered words like currency she could take to the bank, so assured that even in the face of possible death, she could slow her pace and crack a joke?

And how could I be more like her? I was envious of her faith. I was jealous of her peace. I wanted to know Jesus and believe His words with half of her gumption.

Why did Jesus want His disciples to learn from the widow with two coins, and why did He pierce my heart with Wanda's words? It's simple, and yet I think it may be the hardest lesson of our lives—*He desperately wants our trust.*

That day in the temple, Jesus was making it clear: He's not after money or long-winded prayers. He's after hearts that trust. He gave His life in place of our own, and in return He asks for one thing—our trust. Brennan Manning says it this way: "Trust is our gift back to God, and He finds it so enchanting that Jesus died for love of it."[3]

I'd like a three-step process to a life that knows how to trust like Wanda, but as I've prayed and even compared these two widows' lives, the one thing I return to over and over is the reality that at some point, these women found themselves in the throes of grief with empty hands and an empty home. Husbands died, children moved away, friends disappeared, money was tight, and homes became quiet. I believe that in those places of silence, lack, and pain, these women discovered that even when it appeared as though they were abandoned by the world, Jesus was still in the room.

To find Jesus in places of desperation creates not only an intimacy of love but also a willingness to trust even when it makes no sense. At some point in the lives of these precious saints, they began to understand the heart of God's kingdom: He is God with us. He is here and He is good. It's a simple truth,

3. Brennan Manning, *Ruthless Trust: The Ragamuffin's Path to God* (New York: HarperCollins, 2002), 2.

but when it's solidified in the heart, a woman can give her last two coins or walk with peace under the cries of sirens. God is with her. She has tested this truth and found Him trustworthy. Could it be that simple? I think it might. Perhaps we should all heed Jesus's words to the disciples today and *be like her.*

8

A Provider Sees

If you were nodding your head as I shared my memories of Hallelujah Night and dressing like a favorite Bible character in the introduction, then I imagine you might also want to break into song when you hear the word *Jehovah-Jireh*. Most evangelical church kids of the '80s and '90s are well acquainted with a chorus I sang more times than I can count. Let me start it for you:

"Jehovah-Jireh . . ."

I'll stop here—because it is so well known, that's all you need to sing this chorus in your head right now. I apologize.

Seriously though, of all the names of God, I think Jehovah-Jireh might be the one that walks into the conversation with the most baggage or at least the widest gap in ideas and definitions of what exactly this name means. For some, this is an exciting introduction to a name of our great God, while for others, the name Jehovah-Jireh gives you pause. I know there was a time in my life that this was the case. The pause stems from a variety of reasons: wrestling with unanswered prayers, lived out abuse from a church steeped in the prosperity gospel, or perhaps weighing cosmic questions about poverty and privilege. Jehovah-Jireh, which is literally translated "God Will Provide," can mess with our minds and hearts when definitions and methods of provision swing from extremes based on how and where we were raised.

I arrived at college wide-eyed and eager to learn more about Jesus, and although I still gush with starry eyes about this life-changing season when I learned to become an adult and ultimately met my husband and best friends, I did have to wrestle with and unpack multiple moments when I witnessed ministers walking a fine line around Scriptures pointing to God's provision. On a few occasions I think their flesh and bad theology stepped well over that line as God's name was exploited and used as a gimmick to get more stuff. I cringe when I remember one chapel service where the minister told us to stand up and reach toward heaven as we proclaimed, "Money cometh to me now."

So trust me when I tell you that I understand the rolling of eyes and temptation to skip over this name of God. There is a very real appeal to throw it all out when you see the underbelly of mistreating His name. Jesus was no stranger to these abuses, and it's likely He felt similar emotions the day before He encountered the widow with two mites as He drove out the money changers from the temple. But notice that Jesus does not walk away. He loves the organized place where people come to worship, and He calls it His Father's house even as He flips tables and brings it back to order.

I understand the desire to walk away, but I too loved the church even on the days I didn't like her too much, so rather than allowing bitterness to grow, I dove deeper into Scripture,

I talked to Jesus about those ministers who made me cringe, and little by little I was reminded that although God is not a cosmic ATM, He definitely *is* a provider, and He is one who provides more than I could imagine in ways I would never fathom.

Others of you carry less baggage around this name and come to this chapter with stories of God's undeniable provision in your life. You've seen God heal a parent or provide waves of peace in the midst of tragedy. If someone stopped to ask you about God, you would want to share the miracles you've experienced because miraculous moments leave us marked. I understand this feeling too. In fact, if we were sitting down over coffee and you asked about my story, one defining part I would share is about the season when I was the woman in the temple with nothing more than pennies to spare. I would tell you as I sipped my vanilla latte about the three years in the early days of our marriage when my husband stepped out to start a new business only to go years without pay and then watch as it collapsed in the span of a day.

I'd tell you about the weight bearing down as I ran numbers through my head, trying to scrimp and save while my larger-than-life husband shrunk into himself under the weight of his own feelings of failure and disappointment. I know exactly what it feels like to drop coins in an offering box, begging God to help us keep our head above water, and twenty years later, my eyes brim with tears as I can honestly say God provides.

The name Jehovah-Jireh appears in Scripture exactly *one* time. This fact shocked me when I first began to study it. I've heard about God as Jehovah-Jireh so often that I assumed His name appeared in this form often, when in fact, it is found only once, in Genesis 22 when Abraham was instructed by God to sacrifice his beloved son Isaac on the altar. If you are not familiar with this story, let me tell you it is a doozy. Know up front that Abraham did not kill his son, but rather God provided a ram with only minutes to spare. The ram took the place of Isaac on the sacrificial altar. It is a story about obedience, surrender, and a deep trust that God will provide. Abraham walked with confidence up the steep slope, looking up and trusting the heart of God, although I can't help but imagine his knees trembling with each measured step. Real trust always brings shaking to our core.

It is when Abraham saw the ram and offered it as a sacrifice instead of his beloved son that he called the place "Yahweh-Yireh (which means 'the LORD will provide')" (Genesis 22:14).[1]

Interestingly, the root word for *Jireh* means "to see." This makes sense when we look at our English word *provision* and notice that even there, *vision* (or "to see") is connected. This is not coincidence, but rather it points to the nature of God. It is because He sees that He provides. Our God sees from multiple angles at the same time. He sees beneath firmly placed smiles on the days we stubbornly insist, "I'm fine." He sees from the future as we walk with shaking knees and elevated blood pressure into intimidating rooms and uncomfortable conversations. He sees into our hearts, our prayers, and our mustard seed faith. He also sees from high above, knowing what we need even when we shake our fists at His delayed response.

A few years ago, I was training for a marathon with a group of women, and each Saturday morning we would tackle a long run ranging anywhere from ten to twenty miles. One hot summer Saturday morning, we were scheduled to run fifteen miles, and as was our routine, one of my friends mapped out the course. Typically, whoever mapped it would also drive the

---

1. "Yahweh-Yireh" is used in the NLT. "Jehovah-Jireh" stems from the KJV and is why it is more commonly known than Yahweh-Yireh.

course before the training run and set out water every three miles. My friend noticed as she was driving that we would be running through a large park system that had water fountains, and so she made the decision to forego setting out water bottles. Well, as we rolled up to that first water fountain, our hearts sank as we discovered it was bone-dry. We hoped this was a one-time situation but unfortunately found that all the water fountains had been turned off, so there was no drinkable water available for our entire fifteen miles!

Did I mention it was hot? It was blazing hot. I live in West Texas, desert country, where it is common for the temperatures to linger around the one-hundred-degree mark on most summer days. I will never forget licking my parched lips and feeling my dry throat as our pace slowed to a crawl. We were on mile ten as we rounded a lake filled with *very* dirty water, and it felt like it was taunting us. I had packed a small protein bar in my running belt, and as I stared longingly at that nasty lake water, I decided to rip open that package because surely my chocolate-coated protein bar would help offset my desperation. It didn't.

So it was on the back side of a lake with the taste of chocolatey gravel in my mouth that I got really desperate and also a little scared that we might have a heatstroke or dehydration injury. I was running with three women at the time, and although they knew I was a pastor, we typically steered clear of religious conversation because one of these women had made it abundantly clear she was not interested in anything to do with Jesus. Potential dehydration trumps people's comfort in my mind, so as we continued to shuffle forward, I feebly said, "Jesus, we are hot and thirsty. I need you to bring us some water to drink. And please bring it soon." One of the women rolled her eyes as we looked over the desolate road and said, "Yeah, I don't see that happening."

I kid you not, about half a mile later, a car pulled over on the side of the road ahead of us and a woman got out and stood next to her open trunk. As we began to pass by she smiled at us, and I said in a half-joking way, "You don't happen to have any water we could have?"

"Well, girls, I just went to the store, and I've got an entire case of water bottles in here! Why don't you each take one?" Our eyes bugged out and our dry mouths dropped open. We were saved! We each opened that glorious bottle of water and chugged it like we had been stranded on an island. One of my friends took a second bottle and declared this one would be savored like we were at a fine dining restaurant. The lady waved and jumped back in her car. "Unbelievable," my skeptical friend said, and I smiled while also thinking, *Wow, God! You just did that!*

That simple yet miraculous moment of provision has always stayed with me because I felt so seen by God. In the blazing heat, God was at work in my heart and in the lives of the three women I was running with, maybe in the heart of the woman who stopped her car as well. I can't see the situation from the wisdom of God, but as I finished that run my faith swelled, not because of a bottle of water, but rather because I was reminded that even when I was on the back side of a lake, hidden from help, God saw me. He heard my plea, and He smiled upon my willingness to look foolish.

I've learned over the years to pay attention to firsts and lasts in the Bible. This includes final speeches by great people, Jesus's opening miracle, and the first time meaningful words appear in Scripture. Kay Arthur points out that the Hebrew words for *love*, *obedience*, and *sacrifice* are first found in Genesis 22, where Abraham declares God to be Jehovah-Jireh.[2] I

2. Kay Arthur, *Lord, I Want to Know You* (Sisters, OR: Multnomah, 1992), 68.

don't know about you, but *love* feels like a major plot point in Scripture, so I was shocked to discover it had not been used in the preceding twenty-one chapters of Genesis. Without a doubt, God loved all of creation and Adam and Eve, but the writer chose to reserve this all-powerful word to describe the love Abraham felt for Isaac.

The choice to introduce the word *love* at this time highlights the weight and purpose of this specific story within the greater narrative of Scripture. It is a foreshadowing of the sacrificial Son who is to come and the immense love His Father has for Him. The words coming from the mouth of God to Abraham, "Take your son, *your only son*—yes, Isaac, whom *you love so much*—and go to the land of Moriah. Go and sacrifice him" (Genesis 22:2, emphasis added), feel prophetic and reminiscent of perhaps the most memorized verse of all time. Notice the similarities to John 3:16, where we are reminded that "God *so loved the world* that he gave his one and *only Son*" (NIV, emphasis added). And it is here, in this grim yet hopeful saga about the love of a father and son, that we are offered a new name of God: *provider*. The message is this: provision flows from love.

As I was studying the story of Abraham's sacrifice in tandem with the widow's offering, I had one of those connect-the-dot moments in Scripture. I love it when I see a theme or truth run throughout both the Old and New Testaments! Abraham ascends Mount Moriah on his journey of surrender, and generations later, King Solomon built the temple on top of Mount Moriah (see 2 Chronicles 3:1). The location of the temple was declared holy, in part because it was the place where God blessed man's obedience and man discovered God's provision.

So this location detail means that the widow with two mites is standing in the exact same place as Father Abraham stood centuries earlier. Two people standing in the same place having come to the end of themselves, grappling with what it means to fully trust, and encountering love through provision as they stepped out in obedience, offering God their best.

Another first and last detail that the Bible teacher in me wants to return to is the fact that the story of Jesus and the widow occurs during Jesus's last visit to the temple. As I mentioned in the previous chapter, Jesus was boldly walking through the last week of His life and tensions were running high. He'd made points and preached sermons, but the last interaction in this holiest of places revolves around Jesus reminding His disciples through the widow's example that He's looking at our hearts rather than our hands.

It's His exclamation point to conclude so many teachings, and then He walks out of the temple, the place where offerings are made and blood flows, and He turns resolutely toward Calvary, walking with trembling knees to the place of ultimate sacrifice. He is the *provider*, laying down His life, willing to trust His Father, obediently propelled by love.

Provision flowed to Abraham, it flowed to the widow, it flowed to Jesus, and it flows to us today. Why? Not because we manipulate the hand of God with flashy prayers or biblical formulas. Provision finds its way into our lives because God loves us, and when His kids come to Him in full surrender, He can't help but shine His face upon their need. Faith in its rawest form is humble dependence as we realize we are incapable of saving or providing for ourselves. It's the childlike hug that turns into a death grip, not from a place of fear but from a place of love, trusting that the One who is bigger is both good and safe.

So what do we do when God doesn't provide like we think He should? Because let's be honest, we've all been disappointed when He didn't come through like we expected. In fact, both biblical stories could elicit righteous indignation if we chose to see God through a lens of fickle love and wavering loyalties. I could be enraged that God would dare ask Abraham to make that difficult trek, and I could declare that Jesus's watching of the widow looked more like indifference than love since He didn't demand Judas open the purse strings and give this deserving woman some cash. It's amazing how our view of God, which is usually dictated by our experience, completely changes a story. It's evidence to support why we must get to know Him and His true character for ourselves rather than base our beliefs on the latest TikTok theology someone spouts.

When I start to question God as my provider, it is almost always because I have elevated my expectations above His sovereignty. I craft prayers with conditions and clench my fists while pointing to timelines rather than opening my hands in humble surrender. I strain my eyes in search of His out-stretched hand when He's patiently waiting for me to trust His heart. I don't know about you, but I tend to go through this cycle often. I say I trust that God is my provider, but I also really wish He'd consult with me on my plans about how best to provide. I usually have plans A, B, and C for Him to choose from (I'm generous like that). But His ways are higher than my own, and they tend to look more like plan V than my plan A, so I find myself in seasons of waiting where I must fight for belief that He really is the God who provides.

I've walked alongside many people who swing from excite-ment to disappointment when reality looks starkly different from the illusions crafted in their minds. Whispered lies that God has abandoned or at least set them aside while He tends to more pressing needs and important people try to set in and replace truth. I've watched as friends draped themselves with jackets of cynicism, believing that detachment and this know-it-all attitude would protect their hearts from greater frustration.

Can we talk about the trap of cynicism for a minute? I'm well acquainted with the jacket of cynicism. I've worn it myself a time or two, believing I'm hedging my bets against deferred hope when life, people, or God has let me down too many times to count. Cynicism feels cozy for a while. At its essence, it says, "Been there, done that, could probably write a book," and it creates chairs in the sky from which to judge others who continue to hold out hope in a God you assume is destined to disappoint. It feels safer up in the air, but it's lonely up there too.

Cynicism is really just a sophisticated version of bitterness. Leave its trappings on for very long, and it sneakily turns into a straitjacket that binds you up and causes you to lose touch with the desires in your heart. And, my friend, you were created to hope! You and I are both designed to dream with God, but when we decide we know better, we forfeit dreams and settle for mediocre days.

Hope is painful and risky. Life doesn't always turn out like you expect, but hope is also beautiful, and God grafted it into your DNA. God never intended for you to get everything you want, but He does intend for you to discover that He is your provider, and He knows what you need. One way you honor God is to fight for your hope. He asks you to believe in His provision even as you walk up painful mountains with trembling legs.

If you find yourself tempted by cynicism or questioning if God can be trusted, I'd like to suggest gratitude as the best remedy to get your hope back into alignment with God's character. Scripture says we should thank God for everything (see Ephesians 5:20 and 1 Thessalonians 5:18). I believe this is because it gets our focus off what we want and onto the reality that God is good even in the hardest situations.

When my husband and I had only pennies in our bank account, we tested this principle of giving thanks in all circumstances, and we found our lives forever changed. In fact, one day, when my husband found himself at his lowest, he called his mom in hopes she would lend a listening ear and a comforting word. But after she listened to his laments, she said these words: "Josh, I want you to hang up the phone and thank God for your losses."

She actually hung up on him after she said these words, and what happened next transformed my husband like nothing else I've ever witnessed. He recounts that he started to thank God for his losses from a place of anger. He thanked God that we were poor, and he thanked God that we were stressed. What felt like sarcasm ended up becoming honesty and brokenness at the feet of Jesus. He was thanking God for the hardship and for the burdens, and as he lifted his eyes in giving thanks, something shifted.

He found himself weeping and thanking God that even though we were struggling to pay our bills, God provided, and even though we were burdened by lack, we were learning, and even though we were uncertain about the future, we still felt His presence.

What started in anger at unmet expectations ended in awe as eyes opened to the reality that God was providing all along. Thanking God for everything, even the losses, serves as a bridge to remind us of who God is and the kingdom reality that He is enough even when our hands are empty.

He is Jehovah-Jireh. The Lord will provide.

CALLED EVERY NAME IN THE BOOK

The Syrophoenician Woman

Matthew 15:21–28 & Mark 7:24–30

9

A Woman Pleads

Our next nameless woman is in a league of her own (in my opinion). As you will discover, she is extra in every sense of the word. She is bold. She is brazen. She breaks rules, and she wields her voice like a sword in her hand.

The Bible has much to say about how we speak, and it reminds us that our tongue has the power to bring both life and death to a situation (see Proverbs 18:21). No doubt you can attest to this truth. Receiving words of comfort or confidence nourishes and fortifies our souls one moment, while deep wounds still fester from cruel comments or gossip uncovered years ago. And if we get honest, we must admit our own guilt in the word wars. Kindness drips from our lips one minute while venom seeps out the next.

As I grow in age and experience, I've become more aware that rash and wounding words often emerge from the lips of those who are unsure of their belonging. Insecurity, that feeling that no one knows your name, breeds voices that belittle and shame rather than uplift and encourage. In fact, when I'm in a group setting, a sure sign that someone is wrestling with a sense of belonging is a voice that laughs a little too loudly as it attempts to act as a thermometer, merely joining in with what is being said, rather than choosing to be a thermostat and changing the atmosphere. I think Jesus intends a different way for us. He calls us salt and light (Matthew 5:13–14) not mediocre and bland.

Our voices are a force. They determine our future and they reveal our hearts (see Luke 6:45). Our words may sound simple, but they elicit every emotion—from tears to laughter and fear to faith. Your voice has the power to set the world on fire (James 3:5), and it is needed in this hour like never before.

So how do we start using our voices for good? How do we ditch sounding like an echo and instead learn to wield these weapons with grace and love?

I propose that your voice can be found anew, sharpened, and reignited with purpose when it is consistently raised where belonging is always assured.

What if we train and discover the sound of our unique tone in the safe space of prayer as we talk to the *one voice* we will never be ashamed to mirror? The story of the Syrophoenician woman, found in Matthew 15:21–28 and Mark 7:24–30, is a road map to follow as we consider what it means to raise our voices in the presence of Jesus. Her example of bringing both petitions and praise while facing down her own insecurities motivates me to remember that our words (even the less than pretty ones) are always welcomed in the presence of Jesus. Let's learn from this brazen woman.

First, I want you to make note that she encountered Jesus on a day when Scripture says, "He didn't want anyone to know which house he was staying in" (Mark 7:24). Jesus wanted a day off (I'm assuming), but as soon as this woman heard He was in town, she ran into His presence, shouting and bowing at His feet. Her request was not for herself but for her daughter, who was possessed by a demon. She wanted her precious girl set free.

With courage and desperation, this woman comes right up to the table where Jesus is reclining. Scripture does not explicitly say they are eating, but the conversation uses food as a metaphor, and Jesus is clearly hanging out with His disciples, so in my mind I paint this narrative as occurring around the table. Culturally, her appearance at Jesus's table was inappropriate on many levels. She was a Gentile, she was a woman, and her daughter was oppressed by a demon, so she did not belong. The disciples nag at Jesus like testy toddlers—"Tell her to go away . . . she is bothering us" (Matthew 15:23), and yet she presses in and takes a posture of humility. She comes low with burdens and questions running through her mind of what might happen as she dares to break the spoken and unspoken rules of her world. She crawls to the table with one focus, one goal: she is determined to use her voice to find freedom for her daughter.

I can't help but think the first steps into the room were surely the most difficult. Yet she doesn't hesitate at the door, nor does she stand in the corner waiting to be noticed by Jesus that day. No, she comes right up to the table.

Do you find it difficult to come to Jesus in prayer? Do you ever hesitate at the door, battling the lies of the enemy that you do not belong in His presence? We've already addressed many of these lies, but it might be beneficial for you to ask yourself if the lies grow louder when you attempt to pray. The one place where you can always be assured you are welcome is the one place Satan desperately wants you to avoid. So he throws shame in your face, a busy schedule, or guilt if you happen to fall asleep when you try to press in to prayer. So let me pause here and say, it's all a lie. Jesus loves speaking to you and listening to you. He is not aggravated if you fall asleep or only have ten minutes to sit in His presence. In this story, even though Jesus was looking for a day of rest, the door was still open so that this woman could come and speak. His door is *always* open to you too.

Once this woman is in the room, she begins to speak. Her words are not rehearsed or polished. In fact, depending on the translation, the Bible records her as a woman "pleading," "begging," "asking," "crying out," and "wailing." This is a woman who could care less about what is considered appropriate behavior, and she most definitely has stripped off any mask as she bows low in the raw vulnerability of a mother desperate for her daughter. She is undone and fearless. If she were a woman today, I would say she is like many women I know: my friend who continually begs God to set her son free from addiction, my sister who pleads on behalf of a dear friend as she battles infertility, and the woman in my church who asked me the other day if she should give up asking for a future husband.

For years I felt like I was missing something when it came to prayer. I actually oversaw our church's prayer ministry but was quick to give the disclaimer that I was not a true intercessor and was in charge for administrative reasons only. Although I knew intellectually and even preached to others that prayer was simply communicating with Jesus, I still felt like I was missing the secret coupon code that all the true prayer warriors seemed to have in their back pocket. And I knew I wasn't alone. I've talked with countless believers who feel intimidated by prayer. Especially when you stand in a circle, hearts overflowing with "Father God" and "Dear Jesus," it's tempting to try to fit in by mimicking voices or slink away while believing bold corporate prayers are out of reach.

Here is my secret: the more I prayed anyway, especially when I stopped worrying about how I looked and instead just said what was in my heart, the more I discovered that I was wrong about prayer. Prayer does not belong to the elite. It is not relegated to the special few who know the secret handshake. It is not wrapped up in formulas or special words. Prayer is not beyond my grasp. It is not beyond yours either. It is a tool in our arsenal that is appropriate for any battle or wavering emotion. It is here. It is now. It takes time, but it's always worth it. Prayer is a beautiful discipline of boldly coming to His table, pulling up a chair, and laying it all out. Some days prayer looks like wailing, other days it is a quiet whisper, and more often than not it resembles the talks I have with my daughter Haven as we round the block, recounting our days, fears, and what-ifs, a back-and-forth of words that strives to listen to intention and unsaid truths behind the words.

Growing up, my dad led a 6:00 a.m. prayer time for our church five days a week. He fell in love with prayer and knew it would do wonders for others if they started their day off with a set-aside time with the Father. He unlocked the doors of our church in the twilight hours each day for over twenty years, and on the occasions I ventured to go with him (I confess they were few and far between), my favorite part of the hour was when he encouraged people to pray through the Lord's Prayer. This set-aside time always began with his gentle yet commanding voice saying aloud, "Our Father in heaven, hallowed be your name." He would pause at the end of this line, then launch into praise as he listed out the names of God. I remember sitting in the room and whispering my favorite names of God, meditating, and savoring the thought that whatever the day held, I would be surrounded by my Father, healer, shalom, provider, and Emmanuel, the One always *with* us. This is where I grew to love the names of God. I'd watch as desperate people who sacrificed an hour of sleep lifted their hands or quietly sat with mouths moving, reminding themselves of *who* God is.

It's no coincidence that Jesus teaches us to start our prayers by reminding ourselves of who we are praying to, and I don't think it's a coincidence that the first words out of this woman's mouth as she prayed and pled with Jesus were "Have mercy on me, O Lord, *Son of David!*" (Matthew 15:22, emphasis added). She praised His name while building her faith, reminding herself of His power. By declaring His name outright, this courageous woman captured the attention of Jesus, and as she caught His eye, she took another step of boldness into His throne room of grace (see Hebrews 4:16).

In 2016, I was traveling to Nicaragua to speak at a women's conference when I found out my dad would be going in for an angiogram to check out his heart. My dad mentioned this procedure to me but encouraged me to still go on my trip, certain that an easy fix was ahead. I was sitting on the tarmac of the DFW airport and waiting to take off when my phone rang with a call from my sister. She quickly explained that my dad wasn't needing an easy fix but rather open-heart surgery within the next four days. The rumble of the plane was deafening as it began to taxi down the runway. I pressed my ear into the phone, gobbling up as much information as possible, but with a stern look from the flight attendant, I disconnected and the plane ascended into the bright blue sky.

For the next three hours, I stared out the window, wishing I was back on solid ground, shocked and shaken, wanting to be back home with the man who taught me to love Jesus and pray His name.

It's one thing to pray for ourselves, but it's a different experience when you are pleading for someone you love. Upon landing in Nicaragua, I found the nearest Wi-Fi and called to talk to both of my parents. It was decided that I would stay. Both of my sisters were in Lubbock, and I was the main speaker for this conference that had been planned for over a year. My dad assured me he would be fine and that I (like him) was called to preach around the globe. Plus, I would be landing back in Lubbock right as my dad came out of his six-hour surgery. I knew in my heart it was the right decision. I had a sense of peace, but I also really wanted to be with my family. I put on a brave smile and tried desperately to be present even though my heart was 2,380 miles away.

I tossed and turned, fighting to sleep during the first night in Nicaragua. I finally gave up on this losing battle and found myself sitting by the hotel pool, staring at the moon and watching for the sun. Although I was surrounded by palm trees and tropical plants, I pretended to be at one of my dad's early morning prayer meetings and started praying through the Lord's Prayer. I rehearsed His names and my voice wavered when I declared He is a healer, but I continued to pray, to connect and belong in His presence, and then I opened my Bible. "Okay, God, I'm not leaving here until I know in my spirit that my dad is going to be okay." For the next two hours, I paced and I cried and I flipped through my Bible, searching for a promise to hold on to. I was desperate, and like this woman, I wasn't leaving His presence until I received an answer.

Sometimes we are too polite in our prayers. We reserve our honesty for late-night chats with our best girlfriend and relegate God to conversation that is boiled down to a nice formula, saying the words we think He wants to hear. He's invited us to feast at His table, but more often than not we run to that table, grab a little food, but promptly eat it over the kitchen sink, making sure to clean up the crumbs, never lingering long enough to make a true mess. We don't believe we belong at His table, so we keep our distance and try to maintain good manners all while wearing the masks of women who pretend our lives are under control. How can we reclaim authentic voices if we won't be real and honest in His presence? The mask and good manners may feel safer, but begging at His feet and coming close enough to see the love in His eyes will change you forever.

Mark Batterson says, "Proximity creates intimacy."[1] Each of these stories of the nameless women who encounter Jesus speaks to this truth. Sometimes Jesus moves in close, while other times one of these women must take the first step. In our own lives, we have the promise that He is close, but we must close the gap in vulnerability and trust. We must open our mouths because it is in the moments when we find ourselves on the floor pleading that we experience His love and are reminded of just how close He is.

I found my old journal from that day by the pool in Nicaragua. I saw the tear stains on its pages, and I revisited the Scriptures that I scrawled out, remembering how they became the words I needed and the promises I stood upon:

> Steadfast love surrounds the one who trusts in the LORD. Be glad in the LORD, and rejoice, O righteous, and shout for joy, all you upright in heart!"
>
> Psalm 32:10–11 ESV

> On the day I called, you answered me; my strength of soul you increased.
>
> Psalm 138:3 ESV

As the sun finally rose above the horizon, I picked up my phone while sitting among the tropical plants and I FaceTimed my dad. This phone call was different from the previous one that had been filled with questions and fear. My voice had changed, my heart had settled, and my words held hope, no

1. Mark Batterson, *The Circle Maker: Praying Circles Around Your Biggest Dreams and Greatest Fears* (Grand Rapids: Zondervan, 2016), 154.

longer echoing the alarm of the moment. I'd wrestled in the presence of the One who holds the world in His hands, and I had a confidence that my dad would be okay—I knew it deep in my bones.

Prayer doesn't always produce the answers we want, but it does always leave us changed. We come to Him with fear, and we walk away with peace. We cry out in despair, and we crawl away knowing we are not alone. We wrestle with His directives so that we can march forward with strategy. And as we use our voices in the welcome presence of Jesus, we begin to sound like Him.

There is a lot more to talk about regarding this story of the Syrophoenician woman that I'll unpack in the next chapter, but let me end with this thought. I've seen a quote online that says, "Have you prayed about it as much as you have talked about it?" It's convicting and catchy, and it speaks to the truth that more good is done on our knees than texting on our phones, but I would go one step further to say this—pray about it and then talk about it. Your world needs your voice. Talk to Jesus. Weep. Wrestle. Sit. Plead. Chat. Listen. All of your words are welcome at His table, so walk on in, stay awhile, and then walk on out knowing you will sound more like Him and the world will take notice.

10

El Shaddai Responds

You would think dodging bombs near the Sea of Galilee would be the only story to rise from the trip to Israel I took a few years ago, but three days after arriving within the safe and secure walls of Jerusalem, I found myself in an Israeli ambulance with a wailing woman, paramedics who spoke minimal English, and silent screams (from me) for God to please get me home! This newest adventure was brought to me by Texan stubbornness in the face of Jewish Sabbath practices. It was a Saturday morning, Shabbat for observant Jews, and our team was discovering that when these faithful followers determined in their hearts not to work, they took every precaution imagined to safeguard themselves against lifting a finger that was not in alignment with the Law of the Talmud.

I didn't realize that button pressing would be included in Sabbathing from work, but apparently it was, and so as we arrived at our hotel on Friday night, we were surprised to find elevator doors wide open, ready to transport guests to their rooms. Stepping into the elevator, we noticed all buttons shining bright like a ten-year-old had just left with a little gleam in his eye at this prank, and after we stepped back out of the elevator like the stunned Americans we obviously were, the hotel clerks kindly explained that the elevator would be programmed for the next twenty-four hours so as to limit button pushing. We would get to stop at each floor going up and down in order to properly observe Sabbath. "Enjoy the ride!" they chirped. Sure enough, elevator doors closed and up we went—floor one (stop, doors open, no one there, wait, doors close), up to floor two (stop, doors open, no one there, wait, doors close), up to floor three . . . you get the idea. It was actually somewhat endearing, inspiring even, the first ride up, but after two or three rides on this extended elevator, I decided this was an opportunity to become the ultimate stair master.

Apparently, I was not the only team member who decided that the marble staircase was a better option than riding the never-ending elevator, because on Saturday morning as I trudged down the stairs I heard a crash followed by gasps, cries, and then nonstop wails. I sprinted down the staircase only to discover Barbara, a sweet, mild-mannered, retired schoolteacher, sprawled at an unfortunate angle at the bottom of the stairs. She was clearly hurt and explained through her sobs that the pain was in her shoulder. We felt certain we should not move her, so Josh ran to get help as I knelt by her side, trying and failing to comfort her.

I was not only worried about Barbara, but I was also shocked and a little angry that she had even attempted to take the stairs. Barbara was in her seventies *and* she'd had a hip replacement a couple months before the trip. We almost hadn't let her go because of worries about her mobility, but she met me in my office with a doctor's note and the assurance that she would take it easy and even sit out a day if touring became too taxing. But here we were, making a scene as we sat on the marble staircase waiting for paramedics to arrive. I'm certain Barbara could feel my frustration and concern as I rubbed her back while handing her tissues. Through tears and hiccups, she did her best to explain that she had tried to obey the guidelines and she had tried to be patient and wait on the never-ending elevator, but by golly, she knew she was tough at the core and surely she could make it down a few measly stairs instead of wasting her time waiting.

In hindsight, I totally get Barbara. Many detours or tumbles in my life are typically the result of either my being too impatient to wait on God's timing and creating my own mess or a lack of persistence where I throw up my hands, giving up before breakthrough comes my way.

Patience and persistence are opposing sides of the same coin. One side requires restraint while the other asks for gumption, and at the core of both is an issue of belief.

Do you believe God?

Now notice, I did not say, "Do you believe *in* God?" Because that one is easy for believers to answer. Yes, of course I believe in God! But the heart question is, "Do you believe God?" Do you believe what He says, and do you believe that He is who He says that He is?

Let me ask you this:

Do you believe God is power? Do you believe He is more than enough? Do you believe He is sufficient? Do you believe He is sufficient for you?

The Syrophoenician woman who came boldly to Jesus's table had a belief not just *in* Jesus but a genuine revelation and conviction that Jesus was powerful enough to heal her daughter, even though she had not seen Him heal a Gentile before. Let that sink in for a minute. She was asking for something she had never witnessed, and yet her belief was not in the result she desired but in the man before whom she stood.

Her belief in His power gave her the courage to persist in a way that should inspire us all. You see, after her initial pleas for her daughter's healing, she is faced first with silence from Jesus (are you following this trend in each story?), and then outright rejection is hurled her way as the disciples beg for her to be sent away. Jesus finally addresses her, and to add insult to injury, He reminds this woman that He was sent to the people of Israel *first*. She was not Jewish and could have easily taken this statement as a holy brush-off, but instead Scripture says, "She came and worshiped him, pleading *again*, 'Lord, help me!'" (Mathew 15:25, emphasis added).

She still believed Jesus was powerful and had the ability to help. She trusted even when she didn't get the response she expected, and that response would become more perplexing as Jesus then made His infamous statement: "It isn't right to take food from the children and throw it to the dogs" (Matthew 15:26). I'll be honest, this one statement in Scripture used to be like a record coming to a screeching halt in my ears. It is jarring and upsetting when we read this with our Western ears and imagine Jesus calling a group of people dogs. It doesn't sit well, and as a result there are a multitude of commentaries that reach for explanations to try to make this moment less uncomfortable. Some say Jesus's words were a term of endearment while others lift up this story as an example of Jesus changing His mind.

I'm a big believer that when we come to Scripture passages that feel confusing, it is always safest to interpret Scripture by looking at other verses in Scripture. So this is a good chance to compare this story to those we've already studied in this book—other stories of Jesus meeting and seeing women on the margins. As I do this, I see the following similarities:

First, Jesus is at work in the silence. He was rarely in a hurry, and although we want to read rejection into His silences or pauses, my heart lifts a little now when I read about His willingness to allow moments to linger, knowing that His silences always hold purpose.

Second, Jesus was always doing more than one thing at a time. He might be interacting with a single woman, and yet how often do we see His disciples or religious leaders simultaneously being taught a lesson as they look on at His interaction? We saw it with the widow with two mites, the woman with the issue of blood, the woman caught in adultery, and we see it here now. What if the dog comment had nothing to do with insulting this woman and everything to do with getting the attention of the disciples in the room that day? These men, acting like petulant toddlers, likely were motivated by racial prejudices. They were good Jewish boys and had been taught to fear and even hate other races. This woman would be the epitome of the prayer they often prayed, blessing God and thanking Him for not making them "a gentile, a woman, or a slave."[1]

When we look at the entire context of this story, we discover Jesus was teaching just verses earlier in Matthew 15 about the power of words and the truth that it is heart issues rather than race or culture that defile. No doubt these disciples still had these words ringing in their minds—"It's not what goes into your mouth that defiles you; you are defiled by the words that come out of your mouth" (Matthew 15:11). This was a clear reference to Gentiles, and it was Jesus's way of opening the door, even while surrounded by prejudiced minds, to the truth that in His kingdom, people would be judged very differently.

---

1. "Liturgy: Daily Prayers: 'Who had not made me a Gentile,'" Boston College, Center for Christian and Jewish Studies, https://www.bc.edu/content/dam/files /research_sites/cjl/texts/cjrelations/resources/sourcebook/shelo_asani_goy.htm.

These are actually three different "blessing prayers" that were to be recited in the mornings according to the Talmud. Although it is not guaranteed that the disciples would have prayed this verbatim, these prayers are found in the oldest prayer books.

Yes, He was sent to Israel first, but also, He is a God looking at belief rather than birth certificates.

What Jesus knew as He interacted with this woman was that Gentiles and Jews viewed dogs differently. Jewish people believed dogs were unclean and a nuisance, much like the disciples viewed this woman in the moment, but theologians say that Gentiles loved dogs and kept them as family pets.[2] So His usage of the word *dog* would have landed differently for this woman and the disciples. What they heard as derogatory, she may have heard as an invitation. And it is with these words that offend our minds that we read her response about receiving the crumbs as she takes another step toward the table and reaches out to receive His grace and healing power. Jesus was teaching these men even as He interacted with this woman.

The third thing running through our stories that helps me bring peace to this confusing part of Jesus's interaction is the simple truth that God is not afraid to offend minds in order to reveal hearts. Jesus isn't worried about being politically correct. He does not squirm when situations become uncomfortable. Remember how Peter tried to move Him along when the woman touched His garment? Remember how He wrote in the dust when everyone expected an answer? He is not in the business of making us comfortable, and so He leans into the moments that force us to look deeper into the confines of our hearts. He is after transformation rather than behavior management. So here too with the woman, and maybe even more so with us, He allows discomfort so we might come a little closer as we try to discern what is going on.

This is exactly what this woman does. She does not flee or shrink away; instead she believes. She believes Him to be

2. Craig S. Keener, *Matthew*, vol. 1 of *The IVP New Testament Commentary Series*, ed. Grant R. Osborne (Downers Grove, IL: InterVarsity Press, 1997), Mt 15:26.

powerful, and she believes herself to be welcome at His feet. Even dogs are allowed to eat the crumbs. . . .

The idea that Jesus is multifaceted, and keeps this woman on her toes, leads me to see the name of El Shaddai reflected in this story. In Genesis 17 God is first called El Shaddai, which is often translated as God Almighty in English. A more literal translation is "God, the Mountain One." It's a name of power as well as a name of security and safety. Both coexist together. Andrew Jukes has a fascinating study on the name of El Shaddai and asserts that it means "the many breasted One." He explains that this name comes from the Hebrew word *shad*, translated as *breast*, and it paints a picture of a mother bringing her children close in an embrace of nurture and love.[3]

I love pairing these two images in my mind's eye—Mountain One and Many Breasted. I see a fierce mama bear who has no problem showing both sides of her strength, the strength to nurture and the power to protect. We rarely describe God in feminine terms, but as both male and female are made in His image, I know that feminine attributes derive from His abundance. And so El Shaddai is the God of more than enough.

Jesus demonstrates this name as He goes beyond the confines of culture and racial division, bringing healing to the Syrophoenician girl. He is a safe place and a strong mountain in the face of the cries of this mother, and He responds to her persistent belief by extending not mere crumbs but more than enough—complete healing and freedom from torment.

———

Another Scriptural nugget about El Shaddai is that God first called Himself this name (remember the importance of

3. Andrew Jukes, *The Names of God* (Grand Rapids: Kregel Publications, 1976), 74–79.

firsts)—"the Mountain One" and "God of more than enough"—in Genesis 17 during a conversation with Abram. This wasn't just any conversation, though. This was the conversation that took place twenty-five years after God first gave Abram the promise that he would become a father. Abram and Sarai had waited for those twenty-five years and had disobeyed God's directives as they took matters into their own hands, trying to obtain an heir through Hagar.

"El Shaddai" was uttered during this conversation between a faithful God and a man who had come to the end of himself, and the conversation is a cornerstone of our faith because it demonstrated that even after a season of impatience and detour, God had not given up on Abram. Why? Not because Abram was perfect or even faithful, but because the promise never hinged on Abram's ability but rather God's sovereignty and the all-encompassing power of a good God, El Shaddai.

Perhaps you need to hear this truth: it is never too late to reignite your belief in El Shaddai. Maybe you grew impatient and tried to create your own answers because the silence was long. Maybe you gave up praying or persisting because you grew tired. Or maybe you got hurt, so much so that you feared deep inside He no longer knew your name. My friend, El Shaddai sees you still, and like He did with Abram, He wants to remind you that not only does He know your name, but He may even want to change it as He breathes His very life into your tired or weary or unbelieving heart.

You see, it was here, after Abram wrestled with unbelief, that God changed his name. God inserted a letter right into the middle of Abram's name. It was not just any letter, however; it was *He* in Hebrew, the primary letter of God's own name "Jehovah."[4]

---

4. Kay Arthur, *Lord, I Want to Know You* (Sisters, OR: Multnomah, 1992), 47.

With this name change God was inserting Himself into Abraham's name and inviting him to embrace an identity shift. God was right in the middle of Abraham's life, and as a result, even after twenty-five years of waiting, and even after a season of disobedience, Abraham could hope again and stand on the promises of the One who is steady as a mountain.

It's a famous Old Testament story, and yet I see the same truths running through my own life and countless stories of friends. Promises from God, seasons of waiting, choosing control or alternative solutions when we feel forgotten, and then God still showing up and renewing a promise. Along that journey of waiting for promises, whether it be infertility, a business idea, a longed-for spouse, or a broken relationship with a mother, are stories of God refining motives and bolstering faith.

And on the other side of those stories, I've watched loved ones emerge from the fire and the wait with a new name. Of course, it's not an actual name change, but just like each nameless woman we've looked at so far, they emerge with a confidence that they have been in the presence of Jesus. Sometimes they walk with a limp or a loss, and yet they have gained a new identity attached to promise.

As I rode in the Israeli ambulance with Barbara, the echoes of Ms. Wanda's faith and my desire to be like her reverberated in my head. I felt overwhelmed again, unsure how to navigate a medical crisis in a foreign country. Could I believe God in this moment? Not believe in Him but actually believe that His very presence was with me?

The paramedics spoke little English, and I couldn't help but feel they were highly annoyed with the two American women shut into their small vehicle as we raced to the nearest hospital.

They took Barbara's vitals, consulted one another, and before we knew it I found them stopping and pulling Barbara's gurney out of the ambulance and into a bright room with very few people. I assumed we were in the emergency room, and they rolled us into a line of other beds and tried to explain that someone would be with us soon.

Barbara continued to sob, holding her arm and begging God to please take away the pain. A young man who spoke minimal English examined her and then looked at me and explained that I should take her to go get X-rays. I thought surely I'd misheard him. Me? I was to take her to go get X-rays? Through broken words and some bad miming, I finally got the message: staff was limited on Shabbat, so I would need to push Barbara's bed through the halls until I found a room for X-rays.

Off I went, pushing a hospital bed with a wailing woman through the halls. At each open door, I'd peek inside, look for signs of X-ray machines, and if I found someone in said room, I'd use my hands to mimic taking a picture of your chest while also lifting my hands in the formation of a giant X and saying *x-raaaaay* really slowly in hopes it would translate.

Thankfully, someone took pity on our sideshow of confusion and directed us to a room that looked like a waiting area with a young woman at a receptionist desk. Her eyes grew wide as Barbara let out a painfully loud moan, but she assured me we were in the right place and hopefully the X-ray technician would be with us soon. Well, the technician was not with us soon. We waited and we waited, and we waited some more, and during that time, Barbara began to cry in earnest. She whimpered and then wailed, all while I patted her hair, prayed under my breath (*please help her, Jesus!*), and got multiple tissues from the receptionist while also asking her if we could please page or somehow get the technician back soon!

My anxiety was rising as I felt completely helpless. I closed my eyes, took a deep breath, and asked the Holy Spirit, *What can I do?!* As clear as a bell, one word zoomed through my mind—*sing*. As I mentioned earlier, when I hear God's voice speak to me, it's often like it has weight to it, and the word *sing* felt like it had landed deep in my mind with a thump. Only one small problem: I don't sing. I mean, I *can* sing and I do sing, but I only sing in large groups of people, like worship, where I am assured that no one will hear my wobbly and often out-of-tune voice. My sister has a stage-worthy voice, and I am woefully aware that if I lack talent in any area, it is singing. So when *sing* came across my mind, it felt like an absurd suggestion from God, and therefore I immediately began to rationalize it away, thinking, *I'm not going to sing. If this moment could get any worse, it would be due to my attempt to sing. And why would I sing anyway? How is that going to help this situation?*

But try as I might to shake the word *sing* out of my mind and heart, it was now lodged there and refused to go away. I reminded myself of my prayers just days earlier as I dodged bombs that I wanted to trust like Ms. Wanda and be brave, and so I steeled myself with resolve and asked Barbara if she had a favorite chorus. She looked at me a little strangely but then said, "Yes, I love to sing 'Holy, Holy, Holy.'" I told her I thought singing might help take her mind off the pain, and with those words, I clamped my eyes shut and opened my mouth.

I wish I could tell you that a miracle from on high occurred in that moment and I sang like an angel, but the reality was that my voice wobbled and squeaked as I started to sing in the middle of an Israeli hospital waiting room. It was a little painful, but I kept my eyes closed and continued to sing, and with each passing note my voice rose in volume. When I was at my wobbliest trying to hit a high note, I heard Barbara with hiccups and tears join my song of praise. I peeked out my closed eyelids and saw that she was raising her good arm in worship as a tear rolled down her cheek. I felt a peace that had been absent for hours, and at that moment, a man, who we discovered was the missing technician, ran into the room and whisked Barbara back to take the X-rays.

It all happened so fast that it almost felt like a dream, but as I went to take a seat and wait, I heard a small voice say, "Umm, excuse me." I looked over and saw that the receptionist, the only other person in the room, was trying to get my attention. I walked over to her desk, and she uttered these words: "Who are you?!" I assumed I needed to fill out some paperwork, so I immediately apologized and went into a speech about being two women from Texas who had an accident. She interrupted my explanation with a shake of her head and repeated the question: "No, who are you?!"

"I'm sorry," I stammered. "I don't understand." I slowed down my words, thinking she could not understand me due to the language barrier. "My name is Paige, and I am leading a tour group . . ."

"No, no, no. Who are you?! Are you Christian or Jewish?" she asked.

"Oh! Well, I'm a Christian," I replied.

She turned her head to the side and then said these words: "You come in here with the crying woman. She cries very much and very loud."

"Yes." I agreed with a slight smile and nod of my head.

"And she cries for a very long time."

"Yes."

"And then, you sing, and it's not so good, but she stops crying . . . and I feel something . . . and you are Christian?" She was grasping for words as tears came into her eyes and she shook her head.

I nodded as she spoke and simply said, "Yes, I am a Christian, and I think what you felt was God's presence. His peace and His power. He was reminding us that He is with us, and that gave Barbara strength."

She looked at me, and then she began to tell me her story. This young receptionist, who I would guess was in her early twenties, explained that she had become a Christian just a couple weeks before. This was a major life change, as most people in Israel are Jewish and Christianity is often persecuted. She did not make this decision lightly, but the night before, she found herself in a fierce argument with her family, who were pressuring her to abandon this new faith in Jesus.

With tears in her eyes, she said, "I told Jesus last night, *if you are real, I need to see your power.*" She looked me in the eye and said, "And then *you* walk in with the crying woman . . . and your not-so-good singing . . . and I feel it. I feel His power."

I felt it too! In fact, tears spring to my eyes as I remember this moment and still marvel at God's plan to use a wailing woman and my wobbly voice to strengthen this precious Israeli woman's faith. Yet, isn't that like God? He surprises, occasionally offends, and definitely delights in using the foolish things (or people) in ways we could never plan or imagine to bring glory to His name. The story of the Syrophoenician woman begging for crumbs is one such story that surprises and yet also inspires. She teaches us to persist (like my Israeli friend) and believe that *if God is real, we can see His power*! She did not allow her labels to limit her access to His power but instead believed in His name regardless of how those around her responded.

What is it that brings out your persistent spirit? For this woman it was her daughter, while for me on that fateful day in Israel it was remembering how much I wanted to believe like Wanda. So many of us have bought into the lie that a tenacious spirit is a personality trait rather than a right as daughters of the King. Like Abraham, we have received the breath of God into our very names because Jesus is alive within, and the same Jesus who rose from the grave is at work within your life! Walking out our belief with a relentless spirit is tough. Like my journey through that hospital, it is littered with overcoming obstacles, translating directions, and stretching our faith to believe El Shaddai really does see and care.

And Jesus has no problem with stretching or even "offending" our minds if it means we will dig a little deeper or trust a little further or open our mouths to sing when we've believed our whole lives that our voice does not belong. He loves to partner with our weakness and our bravery to answer midnight prayers, bring freedom to children, and create more in our lives than we can imagine.

He is El Shaddai, more than enough. I dare you to believe God today.

BY ANY OTHER NAME

The Sinful Woman
Who Anointed Jesus

Luke 7:36–50

11

A Woman Worships

As we've looked at the nameless women so far, I'm certain you've seen the recurring theme of Jesus seeing each one as unique and worthy of His time and gaze. It's at His core to see us, but unfortunately, we don't always see Him in return. The story up next stands out because it speaks of a woman who sees Jesus and without uttering a single word ministers to the vulnerable places of His heart.

Most translations headline this story found in Luke 7:36–50 "Jesus anointed by the sinful woman." She's sometimes referred to as the woman with the alabaster jar, although there are two different women who bring alabaster jars to anoint Him (the other is Mary of Bethany, sister of Lazarus), and this is clearly a different woman, a sinful woman. This encounter takes place at the home of Simon the Pharisee, who throws a lavish feast that all are invited to attend. It would have been typical for a man in his position to host dinners like this on occasion, where honored guests reclined and ate first while the less fortunate sat against a wall watching the feast and then eating the leftovers.

Ann Spangler says this would be "a way to display generosity to the less fortunate,"[1] and good Pharisees tried to get points with the people and look benevolent when they could.

Jesus was one of the honored guests, although honored isn't how I'd describe His welcome. This encounter took place early in His ministry, and the invitation was more than likely an opportunity for the Pharisees to take a closer look at this man who was causing excitement among the people. We see later in the story that Simon says to himself, "If this man were a prophet" (Luke 7:39), alluding to the fact that he was inspecting Jesus and finding Him wanting.

Hospitality was and still is an important part of Middle Eastern culture. I received more kisses on the cheek and drank more steaming sweet tea than I can recount when I visited the nation of Jordan a few years ago. We were visiting the homes of refugees from surrounding countries, and I remember being humbled by the kindness of strangers who had so little yet gave so freely. When praising our new Middle Eastern friends about this over-the-top hospitality, they looked at me strangely, explaining our encounters were normal and an expected way to greet guests. They were in turn shocked to hear my descriptions of hospitality in the US. I did my best to put us in a favorable light, but when I explained overstuffed calendars and friends scheduling lunches or coffee dates sometimes months in advance, their eyes widened in horror, and I realized we had much to learn from their prioritized lives of open doors and warm homes. Hospitality was a way for them to hold on to identity. They had been driven from their homes, yet they still prized the traditions and value of honor. It was beautiful.

1. Ann Spangler, *Wicked Women of the Bible* (Grand Rapids: Zondervan, 2015), 180.

This sense of honor through hospitality was true of Jesus's time too. Think of Martha and her displeasure at Mary, who sat at Jesus's feet, while she was busy preparing the meal and likely washing those dusty feet. Yes, she gets a bad rap for her distracted heart, but notice Jesus does not correct her serving, only her motivation. Later, Martha is found serving Jesus again without censure or correction (see John 12:2). Hospitality from a thankful heart became a beautiful way Martha honored Jesus.

So as we dive into the story of the sinful woman who anoints Jesus, we need to first take note of the fact that Martha would be appalled at how Jesus was welcomed into Simon the Pharisee's home. Middle Eastern tradition of that time would expect the following actions from the host of a banquet:

A kiss of greeting, usually on the cheek

Water and towel to wash dusty feet

Olive oil brought around for the washing of hands

Occasionally a nicer oil to anoint the head and provide a nice aroma before the meal

The fact that Jesus is not offered a single one of these standard greetings would "be a calculated and pointed insult" according to Kenneth Bailey in *Jesus Through Middle Eastern Eyes*.[2] He goes on to explain that in response to this social snub, Jesus actually elevates the tension in the room as He walks over to the couch and reclines. His act of reclining is the equivalent of stirring the pot, because the first person to recline was typically the eldest or most important person in the room.[3] We know Jesus was in His early thirties, so it's

2. Kenneth Bailey, *Jesus Through Middle Eastern Eyes: Cultural Studies in the Gospels* (Downers Grove: IVP Academic, 2008), 243.
3. Bailey, *Jesus Through Middle Eastern Eyes*, 243–244.

unlikely He was the oldest, and the lack of hospitality makes it clear that Simon did not view Jesus as the most important person in the room—but Jesus still took His rightful seat and undoubtedly caused a stir.

The lack of traditional greeting shown by Simon was the equivalent to public humiliation, and this disgrace was on display for not only the Pharisees in the room but also the mass of ordinary people along the walls, waiting to eat. Jesus was humiliated in front of an entire village, and one woman, sitting against the wall, was heartbroken if not outraged.

For years I thought this woman began to cry because she was so undone by her shame and sin, but after closer research, I've come to believe her tears were the result of her love and desire to give Jesus the honor due His name. You see, she had come to this dinner on a mission. Scripture says she had heard He was eating there, and so she brought her alabaster jar filled with expensive perfume (Luke 7:37). The Bible doesn't say exactly what her plan was, but she sat along the wall with other people deemed less than and waited for a moment when she could offer her praise.

She was known as a sinful woman, but the way Jesus talks about her later makes it clear her sins have already been forgiven (Luke 7:47). We don't know *when* she asked for forgiveness, but we discover her life of sin has already been transformed, as she showed up not as a woman looking for absolution but as a woman who wanted to say thank you and lavish Jesus with her best—her finest oil kept in an alabaster jar.

But before she got the chance to speak to Him, she witnessed the religious leaders of her community belittle and humiliate Him. Did they not know who just walked into this room? She was used to being the one who was sneered at, pushed aside, and shamed, but it felt different when those same scornful eyes were directed His way. He deserved their best, her best, and as she watched this drama unfold, I picture tears beginning to spill from her eyes. I don't know about you, but when I witness injustice, tears often threaten my eyes as well. She wanted to make right what was so rudely wrong, so with sobs escaping from her chest, she stepped away from the wall and came toward Jesus.

He was reclining with His face toward the table, so all she had access to were His feet. She had no water, no towel, so she used what was available, her tears and her hair. She made a scene, and she made a mess, but Jesus didn't mind, so she continued to give all she had in an offering of honor and love. She stepped into His humiliation, His suffering, and identified with Him, giving Him the ultimate worship that her heart longed to offer when she first heard He was in her town.

The Pharisees were annoyed, but Jesus felt loved.

We serve a God who is love (1 John 4:16), and when asked a few chapters later in Luke 10 about the most important commandment of all, Jesus nodded His head and proclaimed that the way to really live is to love God with all that you are and to love others like you love yourself (Luke 10:27). Those words have been recited so often that I think we fail to take into account just how over-the-top this command is. We are to love Him with *all* that we are. The Greek word *holos* translated into the word *all* in this verse is translated in other locations as *whole, altogether, every whit,* and *completely.* Any way you look at it, we are called to love God in a way that some might describe as too much.

When I was a little girl, I could have been described as "too much." I was bold and brave and on the bossy side, but if I loved something, I loved it fiercely and gave it my entire focus. My parents have stories about me sleeping in new shoes and loving my "gonga" until it was a disgusting gray creature instead of the cute little monkey I was originally given. I think most kids start out with that "too much" energy, but somewhere and somehow, we tame ourselves as we grow so as to become more palatable to our world.

Oh, how Jesus longs for our "too muchness." In the book of Revelation, Jesus condemns the church for becoming lukewarm and declares His distaste for the way we are neither hot nor cold. Another complaint from His lips directed our way is this: "You don't love me or each other as you did at first!" (Revelation 2:4). We've lost sight of our utter dependence on His grace, and with that disconnection we've lost our first wild and passionate love for Him. This woman was still acquainted with her deep need and great sin, therefore she loved extravagantly. It's over-the-top, it's slightly scandalous, and it would probably shock us today, and yet Jesus both welcomed and praised this woman with the tearful face and tangled, damp hair. She was willing to look a fool for Him to show her devotion and the honor due His presence.

When I compare women around me who "love God" but hold back their whole selves with this woman washing and kissing Jesus's dusty feet, I can't help but ask, What did we trade our ferocious love for? There is likely a long list specific to each of us, and I'm aware that those trade-offs typically stem as a response to deep hurt and disappointment, but in order to get our love back, I think we need to expose four attitudes we've settled for along the way: cynicism, false responsibility, fear of man, and indifference. These four attitudes have settled around our souls like a straightjacket, trying to suppress a heart that was created to love with abandoned freedom. These attitudes keep us looking acceptable and can even masquerade as devotion while firmly keeping our hearts entrenched in mediocrity when our core longs for more.

Cynicism comes from a place of knowing too much. You see, cynical women were once women who loved too much.

We remember tears and brazen acts of bravery. We also remember the rejection and betrayal of people who were supposed to do better. We miss the days of unabashed love but believe the lie that those days are long gone, out of our reach forever, and therefore settle for watching from a distance, waiting for others' extravagant love to fizzle. *She will see,* we think to ourselves, and with sarcastic thoughts dancing in our head, another nail is driven into the coffin of hope that occasionally tries to resurrect itself with thoughts of *but what if?*

False responsibility keeps extravagant love at bay as it ignores need and focuses instead on whatever task is at hand. It's the attitude of a good soldier who takes on projects and burdens that were never meant for her shoulders. It too remembers moments of joy when love was easy but also remembers how true love demands giving up control, and it chooses instead a rhythm of hustle, a cadence of working harder and faster to forget the gnawing desire inside for something more. A woman weighed down by false responsibility holds tightly to both pride and anxiety, believing that if she actually stops at His feet to show some love, the world she has carefully constructed might tumble to the ground.

Indifference and fear of man are two sides of the same coin. One acts as if it doesn't care what anyone thinks, while the other jumps through hoops to gain approval from everyone. Both leave us feeling lost and disconnected from what is true. If we become fully entrenched in either of these options, we eventually lose touch with what we actually feel and believe for ourselves. It is exhausting to remain uninterested, and it is confusing to swap out masks like lipstick when we need to perform for a new crowd. And yet, we believe that these ways are easier and therefore cling to these performances to protect our hearts from impending disappointment.

The center of all four of these attitudes is self. They are designed for self-protection and keeping anyone and anything at arm's length. We talked earlier about lowering our walls in order to receive love, but we must also lower our walls so that we can step into our true calling as daughters who see Jesus and lavish Him with love. We were not created to be lukewarm or mediocre. We were not created to fit in with the crowd or do everything by the book. We were created to be women who make scenes. We were created to be women who see—who see Jesus and His desire for praise. We were created to be women who see people—the bent over and the lonely, the girl who needs a new coat, and the friend who needs a listening ear. We were created to be women who take shaky steps toward Jesus, who bend down and enter into His suffering. We were created to wash His feet and linger in His presence.

What can we learn from this woman to help us reclaim our identity as women who worship? First, we repent. She had already repented of her sin and shaken off her shame, and although we may have prayed a sinner's prayer decades ago, there is likely something we need to turn our backs on today so we can face Jesus fully and completely. Repent from the bitterness. Repent from the ways you snubbed Jesus when He knocked on the door of your heart. Repent from choosing others and performing for their fickle love rather than meeting His gaze with open hands.

Second, embrace your need and befriend humility. Andrew Murray writes, "Humility is nothing but the disappearance of self in the vision that God is all."[4] Humility is our complete dependence on Him. It does not mean we are weak or frail, but it recognizes daily that He is God and He knows best. Humility takes each disappointment or unexpected turn and

---

4. Andrew Murray, *Humility: The Journey Toward Holiness* (Bloomington, MN: Bethany House, 2001), 63.

chooses to look to Him for answers rather than retreat into old patterns of protection.

Humility is powerful because it leads to true worship. As we bow low in our own estimation, we reorient our gaze from lingering on self to focusing on God's greatness. Like this woman along the wall, humility invites us to see God, and when we see, really see, the beauty of His perfection, our spirits can't help but reach out with praise. Worship is built into our DNA, and true worship is costly. For this woman, she brought her most precious possession, her alabaster jar with costly oil. I think she intended to give it as a gift or anoint His head and hands, but when she witnessed His ridicule, she broke it wide open and poured it upon His feet. She is an example of choosing Jesus above all else. She lived out the powerful truth that when we bring our whole selves and the things we hold dear to His feet, it may appear to others as foolish or too much, but it is a sweet aroma rising up to God (see 2 Corinthians 2:14–15). And it is in the lowly, sometimes dusty places of worship and surrender where we find peace, for it is here, at His feet, that we discover we are no longer seen by the sins of our past but through His eyes of forgiveness and love. Can I ask, When was the last time you worshiped with your whole heart? When was the last time you found yourself pouring out your fears and joy and hopes at His feet? When was the last time you allowed yourself the space to linger without agenda?

This kind of humility, a bowing low and gazing at Him above all else, is difficult. Years ago, when I faced a snub from someone I looked up to, I'll never forget lamenting to my mother-in-law only to receive the following words of advice from her. "Paige, embrace every moment of humiliation as an opportunity to grow in humility." We talked more about this, and she encouraged me to stop wallowing and instead accept my lowliness. This is completely countercultural. I want to rise up and shake my fist when I get knocked down, but I'm learning there is a better way to stand up.

James writes about it in his fourth chapter:

> *So humble yourselves before God.* Resist the devil, and he will flee from you. *Come close to God, and God will come close to you.* Wash your hands, you sinners; purify your hearts, for your loyalty is divided between God and the world. Let there be tears for what you have done. Let there be sorrow and deep grief. Let there be sadness instead of laughter, and gloom instead of joy. *Humble yourselves before the Lord, and he will lift you up in honor.*
>
> James 4:7–10, emphasis added

As this sinful woman was making a scene, Jesus called over Simon the Pharisee and began to teach. First, He shared a parable about how those who have been forgiven much know how to love much, and then He said these words: "*Look* at this woman kneeling here" (Luke 7:44, emphasis added). He then went on to praise every action of love and honor she lavished upon His feet in comparison with this "righteous man's" lack of basic hospitality. She was lifted up in honor by Jesus Himself in front of her entire village. She used to be considered the extreme sinner, but now she was praised as the ultimate worshiper. She received a complete name change and reputation swap.

She was created to worship, to love, to lavish Him with praise. You and I were created with that goal in mind too. Yes, we have unique purposes and plans, but we discover those details and are lifted into places of influence when we are willing to start low, embrace humility, enter into His suffering, dare to be too much, and linger at His feet. The world wants us to think it's humiliating down there, but it's actually the foundation for true peace and honor.

12

The God of Peace Validates

If peace were something you could bottle up and sell, we would have a new billionaire on our hands because I don't know anyone who isn't reaching out in search of peace. On the surface we all have problems that steal our peace—the car breaks down, your child gets sick in the middle of Target, you lie awake at night trying to reconcile your bills, or your coworker makes a passive-aggressive remark that you agonize over in your mind. And under the surface, we are carrying anxiety about the world and our safety, doubts about God, and fears we are afraid to voice. It's a lot to carry, and as the load gets heavier, peace seems to slip away like a balloon floating into the sky, never to be found again.

I think this is why we run after small elixirs of distraction that give us a fleeting sense of peace. You know what I'm talking about: a new outfit to make you smile, more hours at kids' soccer games cheering when they score or sit down to examine the grass, scrolling a new dating app in search of the perfect guy, or escaping into a new book or the show everyone is talking about. It's not lasting peace, but for a little while we forget or ignore the frenzy of our minds and settle down long enough to breathe.

A few years ago, I thought the answer to my search for peace might be found in a new house. It needed work, but it had a backyard view of a small lake, and there's always been something about water that soothes my soul.

Over the years, I've talked to individuals and crowds alike about peace, and I'm always intrigued by the fact that most people describe peace as a place. Think about it for yourself. What is peace to you? For some it is sitting by the ocean, while others may say it's getting a massage as soothing sounds play in the background. Still others have told me peace is being surrounded by those they love, knowing all are safe, while others describe naps under fluffy covers or a gigantic bathtub overflowing with bubbles. Although each of these scenarios is unique, each revolves around an environment that is free from discord or dissension.

In the story of the woman who anoints Jesus, He ends their encounter and her time of worship at His feet by saying the words "go in peace" (Luke 7:50). The word for peace here is *eirene*, which means "to join or bind together." In other words, it is the antithesis of division or dissension. *Serene* is derived from this word, and it's very much in line with the Hebrew word *shalom*, which is also translated as *peace*. Both words, one Greek and one Hebrew, connote wholeness, or as my dad often says, "nothing missing, nothing broken."[1]

Eugene Peterson says, "Jesus is the dictionary in which we look up the meaning of words,"[2] and this thought lands true

---

1. I asked my dad where he got this definition from, and he explained he's heard it for years and links it to Isaiah 26:3–4.
2. Eugene H. Peterson, *Christ Plays in Ten Thousand Places* (Grand Rapids: Eerdmans, 2005), 103.

in my heart as I attempt to define God's idea of peace. In the midst of this story, Jesus was sitting in an environment that was light-years away from serene. As we learned in the previous chapter, He was publicly shamed and then the center of a woman's uncontrollable sobs as she tried her best to give Him the honor due His name. His environment at this moment is my worst nightmare. I'd describe it as intense, uncomfortable, messy, and potentially dangerous with enemies and strangers gawking at His disgrace. If I was attempting to eat a Mediterranean feast in this tense and turbulent room, I would be looking for my closest exit. Yet Jesus embodied peace. He was not flustered, reactionary, or distracted. He settled into the mess in order to speak truth to a Pharisee and value to a woman. He didn't need still waters or soothing sounds. He was the epitome of calm in a storm because He Himself had nothing missing and nothing broken. He extended peace to this woman and invited her into His shalom, a place where our insides match the outside. Where sobs matter because they indicate the abundant love and gratitude of a forgiven heart.

God is called Jehovah Shalom (God our Peace) on one occasion in the Old Testament. This name was proclaimed as an act of worship by a man named Gideon who originally described his clan as "the weakest" and himself as "the least" of his entire family (Judges 6:15). You could say his inside view did not match the outside view that God declared him to be. An angel of the Lord called him "mighty hero" a few verses prior to his weak and least description (Judges 6:12), and it becomes an almost humorous back-and-forth conversation as a doubtful Gideon tried to convince a persistent angel of his lack and inability.

The angel's message—that God was with Gideon and calling him to step into the role of leader and mighty warrior in order to defeat the Midianites—was hard for Gideon to believe, but after a miraculous sign and repeated promises that God was present, Gideon's eyes were opened and he built an altar as a way to worship and step into alignment with God's presence. Gideon named the altar Jehovah Shalom, which means "the LORD is peace" (Judges 6:24). What happened next is an interesting story that could be a picture of the chaos of our world.

After God directed Gideon to pare down his army to only three hundred men, He then gave him a strategy that was supernatural if not comical. The army split up into three groups and surrounded the evil Midianites. They were directed by God to simply blow horns, break clay jars, and hold up blazing torches from the three outposts and watch what God would do. As they obeyed God's game plan, they witnessed complete chaos as the enemy perceived them to be greater than they really were, and Gideon and his men stood in amazement as the Midianites began to panic and fight each other instead of the Israelite army. The dreaded enemies died by their own swords, and victory was in the hand of this unlikely leader.

I find it interesting but true to life that in both stories—the woman who wept and Gideon who led—the environment in which they experienced peace was far from tranquil. We read of chaos, fighting, big emotions, enemies, judgments, and fear. And yet peace survived in the midst of the storm because God was there.

When we moved into our house by the lake seven years ago, I was giddy with anticipation about ways I would create the perfect haven for our family. I envisioned backyard barbecues and chats with my new neighbors. We jumped into renovations (the master bathroom was already demolished down to the studs), and I actually let myself dream about what could be in this new home.

What I did not see coming were the shouts and banging of doors one early morning as an epic drug bust unfolded across the street. We watched in horror as neighbors sat in handcuffs and children that my girls had played with were carried away. I also did not dream about having two neighbors who screamed at one another with frightening threats as a fence was built after trust was breached. I told Josh to go break up the fight, but he looked at me like I had lost my mind, and in hindsight, I'm glad he didn't venture into the vitriol and anger. It lasted for months: the fights, the tension, the chaos, and the unknown. What I also never envisioned was the precious next-door neighbor whose mind was ravaged by Alzheimer's. I thought I'd be sipping coffee by tranquil waters, but instead I found myself walking a confused woman into a dark home where her exhausted husband thanked me with hopeless eyes. It never crossed my mind that my perfect place would feel more like a mission field than a cozy nest. Who knew I'd choose to hide out indoors binging Netflix yet again as I ignored the beauty outside my floor-to-ceiling windows? Yet there I was, sitting on my couch, eating ice cream, and neglecting the possibility of this dream because I felt unsure and overwhelmed by what might happen next on this street I now called home.

For me it was a neighborhood, but for you it could be your family, your workplace, or even the confines of your mind. We've all found ourselves in places where dreams are traded for trials. The woman who worships likely created a scenario in her mind about what her encounter with Jesus would look like as she handed Him her precious oil and thanked Him for His grace. I doubt she envisioned weeping or wiping Jesus's feet with the locks of her tangled hair, but there she was, a reality that looked far from her expectation. I have no doubt you've been there too, hoping for life to go a certain way, then slapped in the face with a different reality.

I think it's easiest to lose a sense of peace when reality is light-years away from expectation. Life wasn't supposed to look this way, and so anxiety rises and hopes fade. We glance around, wishing for a "Calgon, take me away" moment, but are assaulted with the real-world obstacles that leave us fantasizing about anything resembling the place we call peace. It's in those moments, when life feels like a raging storm or chaotic battlefield, that we need to remember this simple but profound truth.

Peace is a person, not a place.

The apostle Paul writes that Jesus "himself is our peace" (Ephesians 2:14 NIV). It's not an environment He creates, a trick He has up His sleeve, or even a certain resource available, like a bushel of bread for the taking. No, Jesus *is* peace. He is the Prince of Peace (Isaiah 9:6), Jehovah Shalom, and His very presence commands storms to calm (Mark 4:39).

We live in a fractured world where our neighborhoods and families, our minds and bodies, are crying out for relief. We are fighting against ourselves yet long for shalom. Our culture is so broken that to walk in wholeness where there is complete freedom from discord and anxiety feels like a dream definitely out of reach. And *yet*, Jesus declares with His own lips that peace is ours. It is not out of reach, but He has left it for us as a gift of His presence (John 14:27).

This is why discovering Jesus anew by His many names and in His many facets has the power to radically change our lives. I've stepped on and off the battlefield for peace my entire life. At the age of fifteen, I experienced my first panic attack and bout of insomnia. I've had multiple victories over the years, but from season to season have found myself retracing steps of faith, grasping for the wholeness I know is mine. Over the years, as I've fought for my peace, the primary tool in my arsenal of hope that has wielded the most success has been a conscious choice to change my vision. Like Peter walking on water, we have a choice to focus on Jesus or the storm. Eyes and minds focused supremely on Him supernaturally con-nect us to peace, while the alternative leaves us sinking into a chasm of despair.

It sounds so simple, and yet I know we all understand the challenge in this call. Storms naturally capture our attention. They are loud and ominous, demanding our full participation. Jesus is there too, but He tends to be less obtrusive, simply waiting for us to choose to shift our focus His way. One tip I've found that helps me choose to look His way is to regulate my pace. When panic begins to rise and worst-case scenarios begin to compete for my mental space, I know no better way to focus on the Prince of Peace than to slow my pace, close my eyes, regulate my breathing, and simply ask for His presence. Some days this looks like sitting in my car for an extra five minutes when I know I need to bring peace with me into my home. Other days it looks like turning my office chair away from my computer before I answer the infuriating email. And still other times, it looks like choosing to step out my front door, right into the potential for chaos, and inviting Jesus to walk with me as I look for Him in the midst of the drama.

Just as Jesus paused for the woman bleeding and remained calm for the woman who anointed His feet, He invites us to learn His ways and mimic His momentum. We see His resolve and refusal to be moved by the drama that surrounds, and al-though you may not think it is possible, we can in fact change our focus, look away from the constant noise, and turn with intention toward the One who embodies sweet peace.

And guess what?! We will be given opportunity after op-portunity to practice this quest for peace. Right now, you likely have a list of situations and people who either drive you crazy or make you want to cry. God may remove some of them from your life, but it's more likely He is inviting you to practice peace. Each day offers an opportunity for us to slow down and lock our gaze on who it is that resides within, on He who has the power to change even the most tumultuous of situations. Jesus is with you. You are not alone. Peace is yours because the *person of peace* abides within your life. He does the actual work of restoring peace as you train your thoughts toward trusting Him. I love the way Isaiah 26:3 describes it: "You will keep in perfect peace all who trust in you, all whose thoughts are fixed on you!"

Something else amazing happens as we align our minds with His presence and peace. When we linger long enough and fully release our grip of control, the God of the universe very often gives us glimpses of His perspective on the storm. Instead of seeing only chaos and destruction, the Lord allows His children to see beyond the surface as He reveals hurts and fears that often fuel the fight and frenzy. When we lock eyes with the One who never abandons us, we become secure enough to love those who are stoking the fires of drama, and if we continue to look His way, we often begin to realize that living a peace-filled life in the midst of dumpster fires is actually what we were created for. We are designed to be peacemakers, women who bring His presence into situations, shifting atmospheres and changing conversations.

Peacemakers are very different from peacekeepers. Peacekeepers often avoid conflict to maintain equilibrium, while peacemakers see from a higher perspective and willingly step into war zones in order to bring peace. Peacekeepers waste years and ruin relationships as they act like doormats or speak multiple messages, trying to keep everyone happy. Peacemakers, on the other hand, create boundaries, speak hard but needed truths, and willingly risk injury when they know peace is possible. Peacemakers are called children of God (Matthew 5:9), and they walk in authority because they can see what is possible on the other side of the current storm.

I'll never forget the day I was writing a sermon about the Sermon on the Mount and bringing the kingdom of God as peacemakers into our world. As I finalized my sermon outline, I felt the Lord ask me if I'd actually like to live what I was about to preach. I began to think of my neighbors and how I'd distanced myself from the turmoil instead of running toward it with His love. He showed me that He had given me a dream house for our family not so I could hole up indoors with false comforts and a peacekeeping mentality; He had given me this house on *this specific street* for a purpose! He exposed my peacekeeping tendencies and invited me into the risky but rewarding world of living as a peacemaker.

I don't have a story of a miraculous block party or even praying with my neighbors on the front porch. Instead, I have a story of slowing my pace, praying each day, and watching as small interactions began to build trust. Instead of hiding from angry neighbors, I began to talk to them and actually listen. I invited kids into my home and kept my eyes peeled out the front windows in case our dear neighbor wandered away from home again. And when the house two doors down from ours that had been empty for five years finally came on the market, Josh and I bought it, flipped it, and watched in amazement as a family in our church purchased it, bringing with them two boisterous young boys who delighted in playing outdoors and infused the joy of Jesus wherever they went.

It was slow work and it is far from done, but I now love my little home and all of our quirky neighbors. One day my confused neighbor, who has since gone on to be with Jesus, walked into my house with her hands lifted like they needed to be comforted and watery mascara running down her wrinkled face. I couldn't quite understand what she needed, but finally I realized she was crying because she had given herself a manicure at home and now was furious as she looked at her hands, which looked like a crime scene covered in polish. I wiped away her tears and told her I'd do my best to make her nails pretty again. She followed me into my bathroom as I grabbed the polish remover, and she quickly chose a bright red hue from my cabinet. I listened to a repeating story as I wiped away the old color and repainted her nails the color of roses from a lover. I wasn't sure if this small act would matter much when she couldn't remember my name, but I wanted the dream in her heart to become a reality, and I prayed to Jesus that He would give her heart and mind an evening of His peace.

It was near impossible to fully clean up the prior mess that was on her crepe-like skin, but I did my best and found myself crouched on the ground, blowing on her nails and telling her how pretty she looked. Tears welled up in her eyes as she looked at our finished product, and then without missing a beat she grabbed both sides of my face and pulled me close to her eyes. "I love it, darlin," she said, and then she planted a big kiss firmly on my lips. I'm not going to lie, I was a little shocked, but I also loved it. It was then that I knew something had shifted and a sort of shalom had entered into the neighborhood. He was with us, and as a result, peace, even in the mess, was in my home.

NAME DROPPING

The Woman at the Well

John 4:1–42

13

A Woman Known

Our final unnamed woman needs little introduction. The story of the woman at the well is a popular choice for sermons, blog posts, and songs, because John 4:4–42 is chock full of theology, evangelism, and hope. It's the trifecta for young preachers looking for a powerful message, and I personally love this narrative because it holds Jesus's longest conversation recorded in all of Scripture! Let's take note that it was with a woman, an unknown woman at that.

It's particularly striking that Jesus engages in such a lengthy discourse with this woman when we realize she is not named and has almost every disreputable label we've already encountered in this book.

Marginalized and alone. We read about her alone at this well when the sun was high and the temperatures were even higher. This well, Jacob's well, is still in existence to this day. You can see it if you tour the Holy Land, and scholars believe it was located about a mile away from her village.[1] So it makes

---

1. John H. Walton and Craig S. Keener, eds., *NRSV Cultural Backgrounds Study Bible* (Grand Rapids: Zondervan, 2019), 1829.

logical sense that most women would draw water either in the early morning hours or later in the day, when the sun was lower and that long trek was not quite so brutal. Yet she was alone, choosing to show up when the other women were away. She was on the margins, hoping to stay hidden.

Foreign and unequal. She is a Samaritan. Jesus is a Jew. These two races were notorious enemies. Kristi McLelland writes, "The Jewish/Samaritan schism was approximately seven hundred years old when Jesus came on the scene."[2] The two races bickered over the location of the temple and which part of Scripture was valid. The Jews saw Samaritans as unclean because their lineage extended from centuries prior when foreigners settled into the land of Israel and married the Jewish people. Bloodlines were mixed, and Jews believed that foreign gods were mixed with the true God of Israel.[3] Because of this discord and prejudice, Jews avoided Samaria, and even though it was often a shorter route to Jerusalem through Samaria, pious Jews chose to take the long way and skirt around these polluted people.

Abandoned and shamed. As we read her conversation with Jesus, we discover that this woman had five husbands and was currently living with a man to whom she was not married. Six men have been in her bed, which is why we find her shunned by the community. And yet, I feel like too often people throw additional labels her way. Our culture today hears about a woman married five times and judges her a little crazy, gossiping that she must be someone who sleeps around and wondering why she can't keep a man. In the culture of her day, a woman married five times was viewed as cursed and problematic. We don't know her full story or how each marriage

---

2. Kristi McLelland, *Jesus and Women: In the First Century and Now* (Nashville: Lifeway Press, 2021), 51.
3. *NRSV Cultural Backgrounds Study Bible*, 1828.

ended. How many husbands had died under her watch? How many men had divorced her because she couldn't give them what they wanted? When you stop to realize a woman in the culture of Jesus's day desperately needed a man for protection and provision, and you add onto that need the realization that marriages only ended in death or divorce by the man's decree, you begin to see this woman in a new light. Instead of viewing her as a whore or crazy and cursed, could it be that she was abused, widowed, poor, and desperate?

In a way, this woman is a picture of all the women we've met so far. She is on the fringe. She does not fit. She has been hurt and cast aside. She is intelligent and resourceful. She is brave and determined to survive. She is in want of hope even if she pretends to know it all. Perhaps that describes us as well.

Until Jesus.

Jesus changes everything.

Jesus plopped down, sitting on the well that day, in need of water and rest. John delights in reminding us that Jesus was fully man as he includes the detail that Jesus was weary and tired as He strolled into Samaria that hot day. His disciples went off to try to gather some food, but Jesus decided to stay behind at this famous well. I have no idea if He was looking for quiet or if He knew about the mission ahead of Him that day. He was also fully God, so I lean toward the latter, and we get this picture of Jesus as God/man—embracing His humanity, as He needed water, but also working in His divinity as He awaited the arrival of this woman, relishing the opportunity to change a life and community with one profound conversation.

The woman approached the well and Jesus asked her, "Will you give me a drink?" (John 4:7 NIV). It is significant that Jesus spoke first. Remember, it was highly unusual for a man to speak to a woman, let alone a Samaritan woman of ill repute. Plus, Jesus wasn't just any man. He was a rabbi, a religious leader who would be burdened with extra caution. Kenneth Bailey writes, "A self-respecting rabbi did not even talk to his wife in a public space."[4] So His choice to engage her in conversation is meaningful. Jesus spoke first and bridged a gap that loomed large.

After the opening question, quite the conversation ensued. She pushed back a little on His request for water. She probably wondered if He was actually willing to drink from her bucket, since sharing with a Samaritan would defile Him. He responded by telling her about the living water He had to offer. She was intrigued by His claims of water that quenched every thirst, but when she showed her interest, He told her to go get her husband. In the past I saw this request made by Jesus as callous, like a cruel joke where someone is exposed when they least expect it, but after further study, I discovered that this request was actually Jesus acting chivalrous. By asking the woman to go get her husband, He was honoring her. His invitation to include the head of her home was His way of continuing the conversation with propriety, and it was also a picture of Jesus's desire to bring living water to entire families. This request, however, exposed her shame, and prompted her to dodge His bright light by steering the exchange to theology. You can almost see her brain working quickly as she changed the conversation so He wouldn't dig deeper.

On and on it goes. This conversation weaves and winds and reminds me of my favorite types of talks, the ones that go late into the night with my closest friends or husband. It's the kind of conversation that is built around something good to drink. It's the kind of long-winding exchange where you settle in, and even in the midst of disagreement or exposure of pain, you

4. Kenneth Bailey, *Jesus Through Middle Eastern Eyes: Cultural Studies in the Gospels* (Downers Grove: IVP Academic, 2008), 212.

still feel comfort. You talk with vulnerability, and you feel free to share your real story because something in the air lets you know you are seen, surrounded by love, and in a safe space.

Jesus, by His very nature, transformed Jacob's well from a place of rejection and pain into a safe haven of discourse, community, and commissioning. He changed the way this discarded woman saw herself, and He spoke value to her heart as He asked for help, thus declaring her capable. Transformation continued as He spoke of deep theological truth, inviting her to engage her mind and thus acknowledging the prowess of her intellect. I wonder how long it had been since this woman felt valued for her brain and her service.

I'd like to pause here to remind someone that God doesn't want to use you, but He does delight in partnering with you. Jesus knows your strengths and He knows your questions. He rejoices in your what-if musings and the hidden ideas you have tucked deep in your mind. When the world reduces you to labels like simple, mom, bossy, quiet, wife, flighty, serious, or single, Jesus finds you fascinating. He created you, for goodness' sake, and He knows the potential, even under the abuse and rejection. He doesn't have an agenda to use it like the other humans in your past, but He does want to uncover and set it free so that others might see the good He created in you.

Even in the exposure of her shame, Jesus continued to speak value. He did not pull away at her confession but rather welcomed her into His inner circle as He shared secrets of the kingdom of God, declaring that the time was now for people to move from legalism to worship. He actually says, "The Father is looking for those who will worship him that way" (John 4:23), and I envision these awe-filled words delivered with a sense of invitation as He looked her squarely in the eye.

Can you imagine how this encounter must have lit her up inside?! The well had become her burning bush. It was a haven, and it held hope. A place that soothed her heart, challenged her mind, and connected with her spirit.

We all need an encounter by the well. We all need a haven of hope.

We need a safe space where we can plop down in the middle of the journey with weariness and in all our mess too. We need refuge from the heat, where refreshment and love satisfy our parched souls. And we need those spaces where we wrestle with questions and feel safe to expose our shame. The woman needed it. Jesus needed it. You and I need it too.

And it was here, in this safe space with a woman who felt burdened and unimportant, that Jesus said, "I AM the Messiah!" (John 4:26).

Y'all, this is huge. This is the *first time* Jesus declared Himself as Messiah, and He did not make this declaration to a crowd or to the high and mighty. No, He uttered these words to a woman. He used the same language God used with Moses at the burning bush before Moses was commissioned to set God's people free.

I AM.

He revealed His nature and His name to the woman no one wanted to sit with, and it unlocked belief in a way that transformed her life, and her community, forever.

Unfortunately, it's at this precise moment that the disciples decided to show back up. Scripture says they were shocked that Jesus was talking to this woman, but thankfully they kept their mouths shut. No doubt the security of the moment was broken, but the impact was still tangible. The woman leaves, running off in such a rush that her water jar was left behind. I don't want to read too much into this detail, but I do think it paints a picture of the truth that she decided to leave her past and the labels of society behind. Priorities always shift after an encounter with I AM.

She *ran* back to her village and told *everyone* to "come and see" (John 4:29) the man who knew her life story yet still deemed her worthy of revelation. He revealed to her who He was, and she believed!

Belief changes us like nothing else. It motivates us to go, to share, to shout what we know from the rooftops. And when belief stems from an encounter with the great I AM, it germinates in our spirits from revelation to conviction. Roots begin to burrow in our hearts, and we can't help but want to tell others about our discovery!

I've served as a global missions pastor for over a decade, and I've spent countless hours in conversations, sermons, and training sessions with the goal of inspiring people to fulfill their mandate within the Great Commission. I love the nations, and I'm passionate to see His name known throughout the earth, yet sometimes the more I push and prod people to go and tell others about His name, the less action I see.

I've come to discover that it's only when people have an authentic encounter with Christ, one that transforms them from the inside out, that we see life-giving believers with an insatiable desire to make Him known. When we encounter Jesus, the great I AM, it changes everything.

Have you had an encounter with I AM that caused you to believe anew?

I immediately think of a few encounters I've had over the years when I AM birthed dreams in my heart. The first occurred at a youth camp when I was fourteen years old. The pastor was speaking about sheep, and although I think the message was directed to students who had wandered away from God's best, my heart heard God whisper an invitation to be a shepherd who cared for His sheep. It was this quiet moment when I knew I was called to ministry, and to this day I love that God presented it in the form of an invitation to partner with Him as a shepherd. That one encounter caused my mind to dream big and imagine myself preaching one day to thousands.

Here's the thing. As soon as I got back to my home, I couldn't help but start telling people about my belief that God was calling me to ministry. I told my parents and my friends. People were encouraging, although they weren't quite as pumped as I was. Yet it only took a few days to encounter the first person who for a time punctured a hole in my belief balloon. As I was telling a man I respected about this encounter with God, he looked at me with concern in his eyes and said, "But, Paige, you're a girl. I'm not sure if you can do what you are dreaming about. Have you thought about being a counselor instead?"

Side note: I would be a horrible counselor.

In hindsight, I realize this was his attempt to protect me from the future disappointments he was sure I'd face. And in that regard, he was right. It's hard being a woman in ministry. I have climbed walls, faced critics, and cried my fair share of tears along the way. But his desire to protect caused me to doubt. I started to realize I rarely saw women in ministry positions and couldn't remember the last time I'd heard a woman preach. The dream and belief that just a few minutes prior felt certain now felt flimsy and like it might possibly be a figment of my imagination.

It would take years for me to recapture my belief, not just in myself but more importantly in the veracity of God's Word.

The woman at the well thankfully does not deflate so easily. I'm sure she encountered a few naysayers, but I also think they must have been intrigued because the woman who typically hid away was now in the middle of the community, inviting one and all to come and see!

She was blessed because she believed!

This past Christmas I was reading the story of Christ's birth in the book of Luke. As I read about Mary traveling to visit her cousin Elizabeth, I was stopped in my tracks by one simple yet profound verse. Elizabeth says to Mary, "You are blessed because you believed that the Lord would do what he said" (Luke 1:45). I reread these words over and over again. They jumped out like a neon sign, and I heard the Lord impress the idea that perhaps I had defined *blessed* incorrectly for far too long.

As a society, we are obsessed with being blessed. We sport T-shirts with all sorts of one-liners about being blessed, and we've turned *Blessed* into sarcastic memes and sign-offs when we want to admit that our lives are actually a hot mess. We pray blessings over people we love, and if we are honest, we do in fact want a blessed life. So could it be that we are blessed not when there is enough—money, friends, joy, peace, et cetera (name your litmus test for blessing)—but rather when we *believe* that the Lord will do what He said?

Over the last year, I've put this verse to the test. I told Jesus I wanted to be more like Mary and the woman at the well and believe His words are as good as gold.

I picked back up an old dream, my dream of this book. Over seven years ago, I began to believe for a book deal, because one day on a walk, with tears streaming down my face, I told God I couldn't shake these nameless women, so He needed to open a door for me to tell their stories or take this burden away. As I pumped my arms and moved my legs, I felt Him tell me a book would happen in His perfect timing. Seven years was not my definition of "perfect timing," so I'd allowed my hope to diminish and pushed these nameless gals onto a shelf in the corner of my mind. These prayers to redefine blessing and reignite believing cracked open the door for God to remind me of past promises. He invited me to take the idea of this book off the shelf and start believing He would do what He said He would do.

I also believed Him for ordinary things. It's not just words spoken into my heart that qualify, but the Bible filled with His words of promise and truth. So I believed for grace and peace as I juggled kids' activities, a full-time job at a thriving church, a part-time job writing this book, and all the other aspects of a full and busy life.

I believed for wisdom, for myself but also for my husband as he made business decisions and built new partnerships. I chose to remember the lean days and the promises from God that one day plenty would arrive.

Have I gotten every little thing I've believed for? No. There have actually been a few times when I've started to pray with hope and belief, and God nudged my heart with the question, *Did I say I would do that?* He doesn't promise ease or that we will get everything we want. He says we will have trials, tribulations even, but He does promise His presence, that just as He sat with this woman at the well, He sits with us in both joy and pain, laughter and grief.

I think sometimes our humanity doesn't know how to act around the nuance of God, who is in both places. We need an either-or, and we watch people swing to the extremes: either *all* belief, naming and claiming blessing at every turn, or we find others embracing a sort of hopeless existence, encouraging others to just admit the pain and join the club of disappointed Christians who've decided this lackluster life must be enough.

I don't have clearly defined lines, but what I have are stories, these women's stories who encounter Jesus, take a look into His eyes, choose to believe, and then follow it up with some sort of courageous action. Have you noticed?

You see, belief, life-transforming belief, always leads to action.

One woman stands. Another woman speaks. A daughter changes her life and sin falls away. One woman weeps, while another wails on behalf of her daughter. And in this story, the woman goes. She runs, even. She rushes to the place called home that often felt like a prison, and she invites all who will listen to "come and see." I love those words. They boil down our call as ones who believe with clear simplicity. We are called to believe and then invite others to come and see for themselves.

What action do you need to take? Where do you need to go? Who in your village needs to hear your story? What would it look like for you to tell others to come and see?

As I began to believe God would do what He said He would do, I was amazed to discover how belief partnered with movement.

In the midst of believing for my husband's business success, God gave me clear instructions on how to pray and prompted me often to bring these needs to His feet.

In the midst of believing in Him for a book deal, He prompted me to apply for a writing cohort. It felt like a long shot that I'd be chosen, but I went where He pointed, and miraculously the cohort led to a literary agent, which led to a publisher, which led to this *actual* book you now hold in your hands!

In the midst of a hectic schedule as I believed God for grace and peace, God commanded me to take a step toward a set Sabbath. It went against logic to choose rest over hustle, but His command came with the promise that if I'd set aside time to rest and lay my burdens upon His shoulders, He'd somehow multiply my time as well as my joy. This could be another book, so I'll just say, it works!

Here is the thing. God sees the belief, but people notice the action. Because the woman at the well invited her village to meet Jesus, she is known today as the first missionary. She goes from misfit to missionary, and her story continues to impact us centuries later.

Our stories matter.

Our actions matter.

Your life is connected to others, and even on the days when it feels as though no one is looking your way or inviting you to join them at the well, you still carry influence. A woman who encounters Jesus and allows her life to be transformed by believing in I AM has the power to leave a legacy.

The woman at the well ran back to her community, and more than likely, she was scared as she jogged that distance. She was headed toward the faces of rejection, the voices of condemnation, and the looks of scorn, but still she went. It's supernatural really, but an authentic encounter with Christ transformed this nameless woman from the inside out, and it has the power to transform you too. Encountering I AM creates an insatiable desire to make His name known, because when we encounter Jesus, it changes everything, and we don't want to hoard this good news to ourselves!

14

The Living Water Transforms

The summer between fourth and fifth grade, my family packed our tan, wood-grain-paneling minivan like a game of Tetris and set out on an epic road trip to California. We watched heat waves rise from the ground and tumbleweeds cross the highway as my dad plowed through New Mexico and Arizona. I was giddy with excitement and dreaming of sandcastles on the beach, the promise of Disneyland, and a certainty that I'd likely meet someone famous (maybe Zack from *Saved by the Bell*)! We did not have tablets or iPhones or even DVD players, so we sang along with the radio, competed in infinite versions of the alphabet game, and threw ourselves into my mother's "surprise craft" of weaving strings into potholders. I'm not sure if I'm proud or sad for fourth-grade Paige as I let you know we made over fifty potholders with every color combination possible. It was a long trip, and somehow those potholders have lived for over thirty years, as we still find them tucked among towels and utensils in my mother's kitchen.

On our drive home, my parents made a spur-of-the-moment decision that we should take a small detour and see the Grand Canyon. It would only add a couple hours to our long drive, and my dad didn't know when we'd travel this way again, so it made sense to pop by and say hello to one of the natural wonders of the world. He turned the minivan north and proceeded to roll into the closest town as the sun was setting.

My parents' plan was to find a hotel room, get a good night's sleep, and see the Grand Canyon the next morning. The first hotel was sold out, and so was the second. As my dad talked to an employee at the third hotel, he was informed that any available hotel, motel, cabin, et cetera was a pipe dream this time of the year, and we'd likely need to drive back the way we came for two hours or more before we'd find a place to lay our heads.

To say my dad was frustrated would be an understatement. We were all tired, sunburned, and sick of making potholders. The realization that this special detour was coming to a crashing halt made the exhaustion more real, but it also made my dad more determined to try to make the most of the situation.

"Get in the car," he instructed, and then he began to drive. I remember entering the national park and overhearing his explanation to the guard on duty that we were just going to take a quick look. It was dark and officially night at this point, so the park ranger looked at my dad with skepticism but waved our minivan forward all the same and wished us luck. My dad drove us to a parking lot that had signs indicating we were at a prime lookout spot, and with false excitement said, "Well, we are here!"

We sat in the dark for a minute, and then we jumped out of the minivan to get a better look.

"Wow, Dad . . . it's really . . . big." I tried hard to act impressed, but all we could see was a big black hole.

We laugh about it now, but there we were, the five of us standing in a straight line staring at the Grand Canyon in the dark.

Fifteen years later, Josh and I drove back into the Grand Canyon with two friends from the Czech Republic. As we drove underneath the Grand Canyon entrance during an early afternoon, I secretly searched for what must be beyond the horizon while also trying to keep my expectations low. I listened to the gravel crunch under the tires and my friends' voices raised in excited anticipation when I saw it. We parked the car along the rim, and our laughter transitioned into a holy hush; we felt the power of this grand place as we peeked outside the windows. I remember stepping out of the car and catching my breath at the expanse and beauty that unfolded before me. It was more majestic and awesome than any place I'd ever seen. It went on and on, and as we sat that first evening and watched the sunset, I marveled at how the layers of the canyon wall seemed to change colors with the fading light. Purples, oranges, and reds danced together to create a visual symphony. I sat stunned and in an awed silence until the sun fully set and light flickered away so all that remained was the big black hole I'd first encountered years ago.

I remember thinking to myself at that moment, *I can't believe I stood here once before and had no idea of the grandeur that was before me.*

I had a sense of grief for fourth-grade Paige and the wonder this sight would have brought to her impressionable heart. I was sad she missed out on seeing such a glorious sight, and then I thought about my dad. My dad would have loved seeing the beauty of God's creation and he would have loved showing it off to his family, but he is seventy years old now and has still not laid eyes on what he sensed in his heart was there all those years ago.

The Grand Canyon *was* there. We were standing in its midst but missed out on its power because we couldn't see past the darkness of the moment.

Jesus stands before us today and every day, but do we see Him? Are we looking beyond the disappointment or the mundane of our temporary moment to realize that our *advocate, provider, shepherd, Father, power, peace,* and more is standing before our very beings, offering His wisdom and love and grace? Today, are we reducing the God of the universe to our version of a big black hole? I don't want to look past Him, and I don't want you to only see the darkness when I AM is standing in your midst.

As I read the words of Jesus to the woman at the well, I see Him trying to shake her out of a fog and get her to see beyond the obvious. In many ways His words should serve as a wake-up call for us as well, as I close this book. Look at what Jesus says: "If you only knew the gift God has for you and who you are speaking to, you would ask me, and I would give you living water" (John 4:10).

Do you know *who* is speaking to you?

Do you realize *who* stands before you?

I know, I know, you've heard sermons and you've just read my previous chapters about the beautiful names and attributes of God, but still I ask.

Do *you* know *who* is here?

Right now.

With the very breath you inhale, do *you know for yourself* that Jesus is in your midst?

What I love about the unnamed women we've met is that each of them came to Jesus not fully knowing who it was who stood before them. They hoped the rumors were true and they believed He was special, but it wasn't until they came close that they began to discover just how amazing Jesus really was.

Their glimpses turned into gazes as Jesus made Himself known and in turn reminded each woman that she was not nameless but beloved and seen and named by Him.

To the woman at the well, Jesus revealed Himself as I AM, but He also invited her to receive Him as the living water. He knew the gift awaiting her was His transformative presence, but like with salvation, she had to make a choice to receive His truth.

This story has a fairy-tale-like quality as a simple and forsaken woman drinks deeply of this living water and awakens to newness of life. The man sitting next to her must be the Messiah, for she is changed in a moment as she goes from seeing herself as a social outcast, trying to survive, to seeing herself through the Master's loving eyes as a woman of purpose who becomes a beacon of hope, proclaiming His name to her entire village.

This name and concept of living water most likely sounded foreign to the Samaritan woman that day. It probably rang out like a spam call. Living water? Sounds like a gimmick this man was trying to sell. But living water was not a new concept from God above, and as the apostle John chose to include this story in his gospel, he knew the Jewish readers and believers of his day would hear Jesus's offering of living water and immediately be transported to the words of the prophet Jeremiah.

You see, centuries earlier, the prophet Jeremiah brought a harsh word to the children of Israel on behalf of God.

> Be appalled, O heavens, at this; be shocked, be utterly desolate, declares the LORD, for my people have committed two evils: they have forsaken me, the fountain of living waters, and hewed out cisterns for themselves, broken cisterns that can hold no water.
>
> Jeremiah 2:12–13 ESV

God was using water imagery here that undoubtedly got the people's attention. Israel is in a desert climate, so living water that is constantly moving and refreshing was hard to come by. As a result, creating cisterns was a common practice. Cisterns were holes dug into the ground to catch natural water runoff during rainy seasons. The people would ration this water over the months of dry weather. Cisterns allowed the people and their animals to survive, but they had several drawbacks as well. Water kept in the cisterns quickly grew stale and was susceptible to poison or pollution. Cisterns were a solution for survival but did little to bring true life or refreshing water to thirsty people.

God was accusing the people He loved of creating spiritual cisterns as they hoarded past encounters with God and chose religious performance rather than true connection with Him. They were settling for a form of God, surviving rather than thriving, and God wanted more!

Jeremiah showed up bringing fresh revelation and words from God, but the people ignored him because the previous prophet, Isaiah, had proclaimed things that were easier to swallow and believe. Instead of embracing what was new and alive and true for that season, they chose to drink from the past even though it left a stale aftertaste in their mouths.

God wanted more for the people of Israel. Jesus wanted more for the woman at the well, and He wants more for us today too!

Jesus made a callback to this language of living water as He sat by a well, talking to this woman who was trying to survive a hard life. He knew going through the motions of keeping her head down and avoiding the crowd had become her ritual and her comfort, but He also knew her hurt needed healing and her destiny needed unlocking, so He offered her living water, challenging her to wrestle with what she had known and take a drink of something new. Through her willingness to fully engage in conversation with the Messiah, her eyes were opened, her heart was healed, and her life was transformed!

It's wrapped up here in a nice story, but I know turning from what seemed safe toward Jesus's invitation was a huge leap of faith. He asked this woman to wrestle with her past, her shame, her false religious beliefs, and her identity, but He stayed by her side and guided her through each gauntlet, knowing that beyond the horizon of dealing with her own stuff was a more vibrant life than she could imagine.

A few years ago, my family went white water rafting in Colorado. We awoke early and climbed into a bright yellow river raft that was captained by a man named Morgan. We called him Captain Morgan. Before we took our seats, Captain Morgan explained that the three people at the front of the boat would get *very wet* with *very cold* water, but he also looked at us with a glint in his eye and said, "It's cold, but it will wake you up and make you see the beauty a little more clearly." I was sold and wasn't afraid of that cold water, so I volunteered to sit up front with my husband, Josh, and brother-in-law Heath.

Captain Morgan did not lie. The water was cold, and it did wake me up. For the first hour on the river, I desperately wanted to abandon ship because the water felt like knives being jabbed into my feet! I know this sounds dramatic, but Josh and Heath agree that the water felt like daggers as we bumped and weaved our way down the river. It was *so cold*!

However, as we pressed through the discomfort of the icy waters, I realized Captain Morgan was correct that I had the best view in the boat. Yes, up front was freezing and painful at times, but it was also a lot of fun! We saw what potential obstacles were ahead, and we got the first look at the beauty among the trees. I spotted animals hiding in the leaves and fish leaping with a frenzied joy. The water was alive, teeming with energy, and it pushed us along with a purpose that at times left me breathless and at other times caused me to laugh in surprise.

By the end of the trek down the river, my body was sore but my heart felt refreshed! Spending a few hours in those frigid rushing waves made me believe I could conquer any new challenge or climb a mountain!

It's no wonder that the woman at the well seems to be a completely different person after an encounter with the ultimate living water. If a few hours in physical living water makes me want to ascend new heights, imagine what is possible when we allow spiritual living water to rush over our tired and weary souls.

As you've read the stories in this book, I hope you've had to do a little wrestling of your own. I pray you've reexamined the silences and discovered He is there. I hope you've had a moment or two of conviction where He exposed pride, judgment, or even fear. I suspect you have taken a second look at what it means to trust Jesus, and I hope as you reflect on your own stories you've found Him sitting next to you, gazing with His eyes of love and guiding you through any gauntlet you face.

Jesus is in our every story, and when we stop long enough to recognize His presence, He is there offering Himself, His living water.

And y'all, Jesus as our living water is better than we can imagine!

Jesus has a little more to say about His living water. Three chapters after the story of the woman at the well, we find John recording Jesus making a commotion on the final day of the Feast of Tabernacles. John writes this:

On the last day, the climax of the festival, Jesus stood and shouted to the crowds, "Anyone who is thirsty may come to me! Anyone who believes in me may come and drink! For the Scriptures declare, 'Rivers of living water will flow from his heart.'"

John 7:37–38

Jesus made a scene! He was looking around, and He desperately wanted more for the people He loved. He knew that when He left, religion and ritual would *not* change the world. He was tired of watching the people He came to save settle for black holes when He was painting them masterpieces. So He cried out, letting people know it's actually very simple to change your life!

What does He say we must do?

Anyone who believes in me may come and drink!

Come and drink.

It sounds so simple, and yet I watch as people stay away from Jesus or get busy creating cisterns. They circle back to glory days, wondering if their best stories are behind them. They watch countless reels of flashy preachers with memorable one-liners, settling for secondhand revelation when Jesus is trying to whisper a life-changing truth directly into their hearts. They are scared to challenge the old way of doing things because rituals are safe, and most relationships they've ventured into have left them in a dust of rejection.

I get it. Cisterns are safe, but they dry out and leave us thirsty. On the flip side, living water is risky. It is a step into the mysterious grace of God. It is believing you still have stories to live and people to impact. It is listening to sermons and reading Bible stories, but it is also quieting the outside voices and stepping out in obedience when you hear Him call your name.

I can see what is on the other side of ditching the cisterns and taking a big swig of Jesus's living water for so many people around me. But isn't that always the way it is? We can see it for everyone else, but sometimes we don't see it for ourselves.

I saw it for Angel.

I see it today as I write these words and I think about a recent graduate of our New Legacy Home who was running after Jesus but got distracted by a man with smooth words and no job.

I know Ms. Wanda and the little Guatemalan grandmother saw it for me when I couldn't see it for myself.

And I see it for you.

You.

I can't see your face and I don't know your name, but I can sense Jesus's heart for you.

You are the nameless woman before me today as I write these final words.

Here is what I want to say to you:

I see Jesus's eyes of love directed your way. You are welcome in His presence, and He has all the time in the world for you. He loves you and He also likes you. He is willing to stop traffic and shut the mouths of critics just to hear your voice and catch your attention. He's not looking for you to jump through hoops, be a better woman, or get your act together. He just wants you to pause and notice His heart and His hand are stretched out and open to you today.

Come. Take a step in His direction and notice how you feel. He has everything you need. He is the essence of peace, but He will also fight for you. He is trustworthy, and like a good shepherd, He won't lead you down the wrong path. So take a step, and then take another. I know there are distractions and whispers that are untrue, so remember who you are. You are His daughter, and you stand tall under His gaze. You can turn your back on the other options and fix your gaze on His worthy feet. Just take a step.

Drink. Believe His promise of a better life than you can imagine. Drink in such a way that you linger a little with Him, like you're savoring that warm latte or crisp sparkling water, allowing yourself the time and space to drink in all He offers.

And then get ready because His living water will transform you from the inside out. Jesus promised that those who come and drink will have rivers of living water flow from their hearts. This means you will begin to see yourself differently. No longer unknown or nameless because He knows your name.

You have purpose and more stories to live. Jesus is positioning you to make His name known, and you don't have to overthink this either. As you continue to come and drink, His love will overflow from your heart onto those who surround your life. And like the nameless women of the Gospels, your life tethered to Jesus will leave an impression, so that even if your name is not remembered, your life will speak and leave a legacy of the goodness of God.

ACKNOWLEDGMENTS

I'm the girl who often flips to the back of the book when I first crack open the spine to read an author's thanks. It's like getting a glimpse into their real life, and I've found myself over the years tearing up as I am reminded that all of life is interconnected, and we desperately need one another. So, what fun it has been to write this book and live out the reality that I needed my real-life people on the days my confidence was shaking or the ideas were overflowing. This is my thanks to a few of them.

Josh, you are my best friend and greatest champion, and let's be honest, this book would not exist without you. You knew I was called to write this, so you encouraged me (for years) and then made space for me to write by taking care of the girls and countless details (you even make the school lunches around here). You've covered our family in hours of prayer, and your fingerprints are all over these words because your love for Jesus transforms my life every day.

Selah and Haven, you are my hope and joy! Thank you for being excited about this book and for allowing me quiet hours in the sunroom so I could finish one more chapter. You two keep life fun, and you also remind me of what really matters.

This book is for you. You were in my mind as I wrote these words because I know that as much as I love you, Jesus loves you even more.

Dad, thank you. Your radical obedience to the Lord has marked my life, and I am so proud to be your daughter. Thank you for reading my words and helping me title my chapters. You are still the best preacher I know—not because of witty one-liners, but because of how you represent the Father and love people so well.

Mom, thank you for replying every time I sent you a new chapter by letting me know you were crying. Your belief in me has always propelled me to go a little farther than I thought possible. And I hope you know just how many lives you have impacted. They may not all remember your name, but I have no doubt they felt your love. I, for one, have been changed by you.

Leslie and Kelsey, I'm so thankful God gave me you. Life is better because you are my sisters, and no one can make me double over in laughter like you two. Thank you for listening as I talked about this book ad nauseam and for celebrating every win along the way.

Marcy, I thought of you often as I wrote about these women. Your love for Jesus and your willingness to come close, slow down, and sit at His feet inspires me daily. Thank you for your prayers, for your wisdom, and for raising such an amazing son.

Dawn, Cynthia, Brooke, Gaila, Christa, and Terri—you've all worked with me over the last few years, which means you've listened to my ideas, read my words, and given me the best feedback. You've sharpened me, prayed with me, laughed with me, and pointed me to the feet of Jesus more times than I can count. Thank you for letting me talk about *all the things* as I've stood in the doorway between my office and yours—it's become one of my favorite places.

Erin, Tara, and Christie, thank you for being some of my first readers and for your encouragement and prayers along the way. It's just like God to orchestrate life so that the college girls I led decades ago are now some of my favorite friends.

COTR, it is pure joy to call you home, and an honor to lead in a place where generosity is second nature and the pursuit of God's presence is the priority. Thank you, *Heath,* for making space for me to write and lead. And thank you to *Jantzen, Rick, Dusty, Josh, Robert, Chris, Jonathan,* and so many other strong yet humble men for creating a culture where women can flourish. And to the talented women I work with: *Shanna, Zephare, Lacey, Kacey, Amanda,* and the list goes on . . . you make me excited about the future of COTR.

Joy, I've never met you in person, but you've helped make this dream of a book come true as the *best* literary agent, and one day we *will* go out to a fabulous dinner in Paris. I'm so glad God nudged me to sign up for your first cohort, and I'm beyond thankful for the way you've believed in me and helped me navigate this new world of publishing.

And to the team at Bethany House, I'm over the moon to be working with you. *Jennifer,* when you told me this was the book you wanted your daughter to read, I knew I'd found a person who got what I was trying to communicate. Thank you for making me cut over eight thousand words and for challenging me to make a good idea even better. *Elisa,* I'm grateful for your keen eye and your kind words.

And to *Jesus,* thank You for coming to this earth and making the religious uncomfortable as You went out of Your way to stop and see and speak to women like me. There is no one like You, and when I slow down long enough to think about how You've led me and loved me over forty years, I am overwhelmed and undone. I hope to spend the next forty years living in a way that allows others to know just how good You really are.

Paige Allen is a wife, mother, pastor, speaker, and podcast host. She's passionate about opening the door for others to have aha moments with Scripture, and she believes our stories have the power to transform lives. Paige serves as executive pastor at a multisite church in Texas, and she holds an MDiv from The King's University. Paige is a fan of vanilla lattes, a good book, and West Texas sunsets. You can connect with her on social media @PaigeAllenTexas.